CAPTAIN JONES'S WORMSLOW

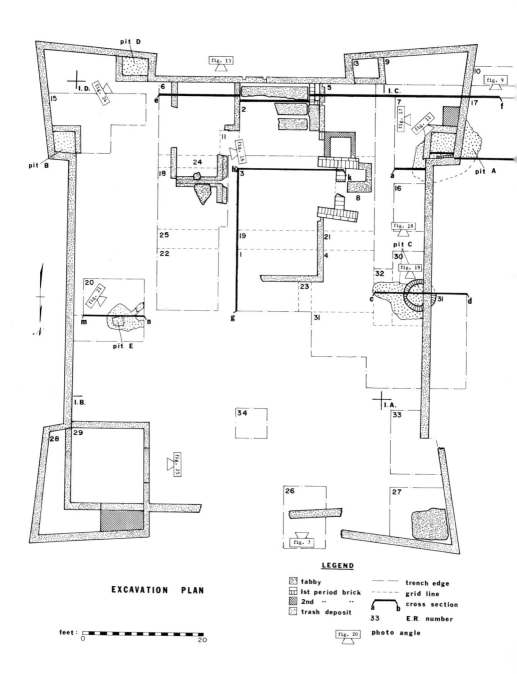

pit D

fig. 13

I.D.

fig. 24

15

pit B

6

e

5

13

9

10

fig. 9

I.C.

17

f

2

fig. 17

fig. 11

7

11

fig. 16

24

h

18

3

k

1

pit A

16

8

25

19

21

fig. 18

pit C

22

1

4

30

23

32

fig. 19

20

fig. 21

31

c

31

d

m

n

pit E

g

I.B.

I.A.

33

28

29

fig. 25

34

26

27

fig. 7

LEGEND

▨	tabby	——	trench edge
⊞	1st period brick	- - -	grid line
▦	2nd " "	a⌐⌐b	cross section
⦙	trash deposit	33	E.R. number

EXCAVATION PLAN

fig. 20   photo angle

feet : 0 ▭▬▭▬▭▬▭▬▭▬ 20

Captain Jones's Wormslow

A Historical, Archaeological, and Architectural Study
of an Eighteenth-Century Plantation Site
near Savannah, Georgia

by

WILLIAM M. KELSO

WORMSLOE FOUNDATION PUBLICATIONS
NUMBER THIRTEEN

THE UNIVERSITY OF GEORGIA PRESS
ATHENS

Copyright © 1979 by the University of Georgia Press
Athens 30602

All rights reserved

Set in 12 on 14 point Linotype Baskerville
Printed in the United States of America

Library of Congress Cataloging in Publication Data

Kelso, William M.
   Captain Jones's Wormslow.
   (Wormsloe Foundation publications; no. 13)
   Bibliography.
   Includes index.
      1. Wormsloe. 2. Jones, Noble Wimberly, d.
1805. I. Title. II. Series: Wormsloe Foundation
Publications no. 13.

F294.W6K44   975.8′724   78–2288
        ISBN 0–8203–0447–6

 *Contents*

Illustrations

Foreword

The Wormsloe Foundation is a nonprofit organization which was chartered on 18 December 1951, by the Superior Court of Chatham County, Georgia. In the words of the charter, "The objects and purposes of this Foundation are the promotion of historical research and the publication of the results thereof; the restoration, preservation, and maintenance of historical sites and documents and the conduct of an educational program in the study of history in the State of Georgia, and in states adjoining thereto."

As its first important activity, the Foundation began the publication of a series of historical works and documents under the title of "Wormsloe Foundation Publications." They consist of important manuscripts, reprints of rare publications, and historical narratives relative to Georgia and the South. The first volume appeared in 1955, written by E. Merton Coulter, the general editor of the series, and entitled *Wormsloe: Two Centuries of a Georgia Family*. This volume gives the historical background of the Wormsloe estate and a history of the family that has owned it for almost two and a half centuries.

The second publication of the Foundation was *The Journal of William Stephens, 1741–1743*, and the third volume was *The Journal of William Stephens, 1743–1745*, which is a continuation of the journal as far as any known copy is extant. However, there is evidence that Stephens kept his journal for some years after 1745. These volumes were edited by the general editor and were published in 1958 and 1959, respectively.

The fourth volume of the series was the republication of the unique copy of *A True and Historical Narrative of the Colony of Georgia . . . With Comments by the Earl of Egmont,* by Pat. Tailfer et al. The original volume is in the John Carter Brown Library of Brown University. In this publication the comments of Egmont appear in print for the first time. With the permission of Brown University, this volume was edited by Clarence L. Ver Steeg of Northwestern University.

The fifth volume in the series was the long-missing first part of Egmont's three manuscript volumes of his journal. It was edited by Robert G. McPherson of the University of Georgia. This volume contains the journal from 1732 to 1738, inclusive, and is owned by the Gilcrease Institute of American History and Art, Tulsa, Oklahoma, which gave permission for its publication.

In 1963 the Foundation published its sixth volume, *The Journal of Peter Gordon, 1732–1735,* which was edited by the general editor of the series. Gordon came to Georgia with Oglethorpe on the first voyage; he began his journal on leaving England. The original manuscript was acquired in 1947 by the Wormsloe Foundation, which presented it to the General Library of the University of Georgia.

The seventh volume in the series was *Joseph Vallence Bevan, Georgia's First Official Historian.* It is a departure from the nature of the five volumes directly preceding, which are documentary. It was written by the general editor, bringing to light the historiographer who was appointed Georgia's first official historian by the state legislature.

The eighth volume, *Henry Newman's Salzburger Letterbooks,* begins a series within the general series, for it is to be followed by several volumes of translations of the Urlsperger Reports (*Ausführliche Nachrichten . . . ,* edited by Samuel Urlsperger, Halle, 1735 ff, and dealing with the Georgia Salzburgers). This volume was edited by George Fenwick

Jones of the University of Maryland, who has also edited later volumes of the Salzburger translations.

The ninth volume of the Wormsloe Foundation Publications is the first of several volumes of the Urlsperger reports in translation to be published in this series. It appeared in 1968. The second volume of the Urlsperger reports (being the tenth volume in the general series) was published in 1969, edited by George Fenwick Jones, and extends over the years 1734–1735. The third volume in the Urlsperger series (the eleventh in the general series) covers the year 1736 and was published in 1972. It was translated and edited by Professor Jones with the assistance of Marie Hahn of Hood College. The fourth volume in the Urlsperger series (the twelfth in the general series) was edited by Professor Jones and translated by him with Renate Wilson of the Johns Hopkins University. The present volume is an interruption in the progression of the Urslperger series and is the thirteenth in the general series. Entitled *Captain Jones's Wormslow,* it is an archaeological investigation of a colonial ruin on the grounds of the Wormsloe estate. The director of the excavation and author of the volume is William M. Kelso, Commissioner, Virginia Research Center for Archaeology, Williamsburg, Virginia.

E. MERTON COULTER
General Editor

 *Acknowledgments*

Initially the idea to investigate archaeologically the Worms-low * ruins came from Malcolm Bell, III, classical archaeologist at the University of Virginia and Jones family descendant. It was he who first interested the Wormsloe Foundation in the archaeological possibilities at Wormslow; therefore it is proper that my first expression of gratitude should go to him. However, without the continued interest and support of Craig Barrow, Jr., secretary-treasurer of the Wormsloe Foundation, this study could never have been made at all; therefore I am indeed grateful to him and to the Foundation. Also, I would like to express my thanks to the late Elfrida DeRenne Barrow, who kindly allowed me the "run" of the Wormslow site during the excavation and whose unflagging interest in seeking historical truth was a constant inspiration to me throughout the project.

I am also indebted to the late James M. Smith, former director of the Graduate Institute of the Liberal Arts, Emory University, whose interest in historical archaeology enabled the project to be incorporated into my graduate work at Emory. I would also like to thank John T. Juricek, Emory University, for serving as my advisor and for his critical reading of the manuscript. I am equally grateful to Ivor Noël Hume, Director, Department of Archaeology, Colonial Williamsburg, for his help in preparing the archaeological manuscript and to James Grady, Georgia Institute of Technology School of Architecture, for his aid in researching and preparing the architectural data.

* Eighteenth-century spelling, which I use through this study.

Louis De Vorsey, University of Georgia, and Lilla Hawes, Georgia Historical Society, were instrumental in locating key historical documents for which I am most grateful. Marion Hemperley, Georgia Department of Archives and History, and Eudora DeRenne Roebling aided the historical research.

My thanks also go to those who assisted in the excavation: Samuel D. Smith, Mary Ellen Schlein, Thomas L. Grooms, Pamela Rhoads, Anne Cooke, Rex Gonnsen, Robert Eason, Meredith Roppel. Bruce King, Glenn Anders, and David Restuccia helped with photographic printing.

Also without the encouragement, typing, and tolerance of my wife, Ellen, this manuscript could never have been produced.

In the fall of 1978, while this book was in press, those associated with the Wormsloe Foundation were saddened by the death of Craig Barrow, Jr. Mr. Barrow was the prime mover in the Wormsloe Foundation for this project and a direct descendant of Noble Jones, first settler of Wormslow. I would like to dedicate this volume to his memory.

CAPTAIN JONES'S WORMSLOW

 *Introduction*

During the fall of 1968 and the summer of 1969, the author conducted archaeological excavations at the site of eighteenth-century ruins at Wormslow, near Savannah, Georgia. The Wormsloe Foundation, Incorporated, owner of the site, sponsored the work for two basic reasons. The Foundation decided that preservation work had to be done to protect the eroding tabby (bonded oyster shell, lime, and sand) ruins from further deterioration. Preservation, in turn, would require a certain amount of digging, and therefore it was decided that careful archaeological excavations would best serve the purpose and possibly would have the additional advantage of yielding more information about the ruins and the way of life of the eighteenth-century inhabitants.

But beyond the immediate deterioration of the ruins at Wormslow, certain detailed historical questions needed to be answered. Before excavations began, historical records seemed to indicate that the tabby ruins were the remains of Fort Wimberly, probably constructed in the mid-eighteenth century by Noble Jones, an original settler and civil servant of Georgia. The records further suggested that Fort Wimberly had been constructed on the site of Jones's earlier fortification, a timber guardhouse known as Jones' Fort, built in 1739–1740. Therefore the opportunity presented itself for an archaeological study of two periods of Georgia coastal fortifications, the earlier built as a major link in General James Oglethorpe's chain of defenses against the Spanish threat from Florida in the 1740s, and the later presumably built to repel the French.

The project also presented an opportunity to test the thesis that foreign frontier environments do in fact affect traditional cultural processes. More specifically Wormslow had the potential to define what effect the semitropical, hostile border, colony environment of Georgia had on the plantation development scheme of at least one transplanted English settler.

After the author had conducted preliminary archaeological testing from October until December 1968, the Wormsloe Foundation provided a grant administered through Emory University's Graduate Department Institute of the Liberal Arts that enabled him to conduct extensive archaeological excavations in and around the ruins the following summer.

As excavations began to uncover architectural remains, explaining why Noble Jones built as he did became the overriding objective of the work. Such a question necessarily required research into parallel architecture of the colonial southeastern coastal region and ultimately into records of early seventeenth-century Northern Ireland, where similar environmental processes were apparently at work on a similar architectural English mind set.

The specific objectives of the project were: (1) to search for evidence of the timber guardhouse known as Jones' Fort; (2) to determine how and when the tabby structures were constructed; (3) to record all salient architectural features above and below ground before further deterioration took place; (4) to determine the purpose of various architectural features of the tabby ruins; (5) to locate the well; (6) to prepare a documentary reconstruction of the site and the way of life of the inhabitants; (7) to determine the extent of previous unrecorded excavations at the site; (8) to inspect the condition of the ruin foundations for preservation work.

Initially the report presents the documentary history of Wormslow. A presentation of the archaeological evidence follows with an attempt to correlate it with the historical documents. Ultimately a reconstruction of the site is drawn based on a combination of the historical and archaeological evidence, an architectural study of the ruins, and information collected concerning early Georgia architecture in general and other eighteenth-century buildings in particular. The report concludes with a detailed study of the artifacts with illustrations, descriptions, and identification of the important pieces.

Wormslow is located ten miles southeast of Savannah on the southern peninsula of the Isle of Hope (see figs. 1 and 2). The original land grant contained 500 acres, the southernmost two-thirds of the peninsula, but since then 270 acres to the north and Long Island, 72 acres to the southeast, have been added to the property. The land is bounded by the Skidaway River, the Isle of Hope River, Jones' Narrows, Long Island and marsh on the east, Cedar Hammock Creek and Pigeon Island on the south, and Back River on the west.

The tabby ruins site is located on the east side of the penin-

Fig. 1. Location of Wormslow.

sula, at the extreme south end of the main entrance road to the plantation. The site is two hundred feet north and west of a bank of a saltwater creek known as Jones' Narrows. During the eighteenth century the creek was known as Skidaway Narrows and it connected Back River with the Skidaway River. Together the waterways provided the only southern inland water approach to Savannah. The ruins are bounded by woods on the west and north sides, and a monument marking the original Jones family graveyard is located about two hundred feet to the east. The present residence is located about one-half mile north of the ruins.

Fig. 2. Aerial photograph of the Isle of Hope and vicinity, 1952
(USDA).

Documentary History

NOBLE JONES'S OWNERSHIP
1737–1775

Noble Jones applied for a lease of five hundred acres on the Isle of Hope in 1737 or 1738, dividing the island with Henry Parker and John Fallowfield.[1] The exact date of the application is not known, but Colonel William Stephens, secretary for the colony, wrote in July 1740 that Jones had "occupied it two or three years."[2] The lease was subject to the approval of the Trustees of the colony in England, but no action was taken until 1745 when a new petition stated that Jones had been at much expense improving this tract.[3]

The records are equally mute concerning the exact date that Jones built his house on the Isle of Hope, but he had a structure there by 6 November 1739, the date James Habersham addressed a letter "to Noble Jones at his H[ouse] at ye Island of Hope."[4] In August 1740 Stephens met Jones at his plantation "house"[5] and by the following February the plantation was described as follows: "[Noble Jones] has erected what very justly (when finished) may be called a good house with convenient Out-houses for Servants, Cattle, and ca. he has also fenced and brought into tillage about 14 acres of Land, he appears very industrious, the Land is of the best kind, and has produced very well."[6] Apparently Jones finished the house by 1745. During that year Edward Kimber published a series of articles in *London Magazine* entitled "Itinerant Observations in America." Kimber's description of his visit to "the Settlement of Mr. Jones" provides the only substantial narrative on the appearance of the plantation:

We arrived [from St. Catherine's Island] in somewhat more than two Days at the *Narrows,* where there is a Kind of *Manchecolas* Fort for their Defence, garison'd from Wormsloe where we soon arriv'd. It is the settlement of Mr. Jones, 10 Miles S.E. of *Savannah,* and we could not help observing, as we passed, several pretty Plantations. *Wormsloe* is one of the most agreeable Spots I ever saw, and the improvements of that ingenious Man are very extraordinary: He commands a Company of Marines, who are quartered in Huts near his House, which is also a tolerable defensible Place with small Arms. From this House there is a Vista of near three Miles, cut thro' the woods to Mr. Whitefield's Orphan House, which has a very fine Effect on the sight.[7]

A footnote to the article states that Kimber wrote in early 1743, but earlier pages contain a description of a powder magazine explosion at Frederica in 1744. It is therefore reasonable to conclude that Kimber wrote the Wormslow description sometime between the date of the explosion in 1744 and the year of publication in London, 1745.

The Kimber description mentions or implies several important facts about Wormslow: (1) it was an "extraordinary" plantation compared with the several "pretty Plantations" along the way from St. Catherines; (2) the house was fortified being "tolerable defensible with small arms"; (3) huts for the marines existed near the house; (4) there was a clearing through the woods from the house to Bethesda; (5) there was a manchecolas (blockhouse type) fort nearby on the water.

What Kimber means by his general narrative is made clearer by a map (fig. 3) drawn by William Gerard DeBrahm, Royal Engineer for the colonies of South Carolina, Florida, and Georgia in late 1751 or early 1752, submitted to the Secretary of the Colony of Georgia at Savannah on 24 March 1752.[8] Part of the map shows the Isle of Hope and the Skidaway Narrows area complete with the names of the plantation owners, apparently all of their important plantation buildings, and the outline of their cleared lands. On the Nar-

rows, DeBrahm shows the plantations of "Mr. Cornel :
Stewen" (William Stephens), "Mr. Withefield's Orphan
Haus" (Whitfield's Orphan House or Bethesda), "Cap :
Jones" (Noble Jones), and "Henry Parker, esq : Prasident"
(president of the colony, 1750–1752). The map clearly locates Noble Jones's plantation directly on the Narrows (the
exact location of the tabby ruins at Wormsloe today), the
vista mentioned by Kimber "cut thro' the woods to Mr.
Whitefield's Orphan House" and the shape of the Jones's
settlement enclosure, a four-bastioned, walled structure identical to the tabby ruin plan at Wormsloe today. No other
structures are shown on Jones's property, whereas the main
house and outbuildings are shown for Stephens's property
and Bethesda. Therefore it can be assumed that the bastioned
structure labeled "Cap : Jones," the only structure shown
on Jones's land, and his plantation are one in the same. Such
an unusual structure probably inspired Kimber's remarks:

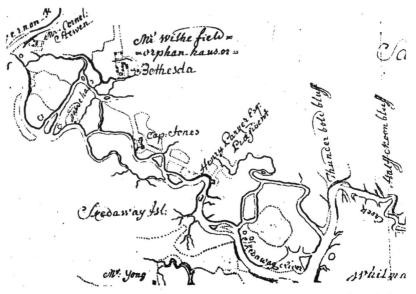

Fig. 3. Detail of DeBrahm map of the Isle of Hope and vicinity,
1752 (Library of Congress).

the "extraordinary" improvements "of that ingenious man [Jones] . . . tolerable defensible with small arms." [9] Not only did DeBrahm show Jones's plantation structure and the clearings, but he also included the "gard haus" (guard-house) location, probably the "Manchecolas Fort" mentioned by Kimber. However, DeBrahm locates the building on an island (modern Pigeon Isle) one and one-fourth miles down the Narrows from the bastioned structure of "Cap: Jones."

Other records are confusing concerning when and where the guardhouse was built. Sometime in late 1739 or the first half of 1740, Oglethorpe ordered Noble Jones "to raise ten men for a Guard & Scout Boat." [10] The exact date of the order for a guard at the Narrows is uncertain. According to Oglethorpe's account book, Noble Jones and his ten marines were paid on 21 March 1740 for the previous seven months (from August 1739 to March 1740) while Oglethorpe's orders establishing the command are dated August 1740. [11] The construction date of a guardhouse, headquarters for the scout boat, is equally confusing. In August 1740 Stephens mentioned that the guardhouse was "a mile or two distance" from Jones's plantation house, and Jones and Stephens "went together to the Watch-House, which I found in pretty good order; but with little more Expence and Labour, it would be very useful and capable of Annoyance and Defense." [12] Moreover, on 29 September 1740 the treasurer of the colony, Thomas Jones, was allotted 27£ 18s 6p to cover "the charges of the Building a Guard House on Pine Island near Skidaway Narrows." [13] But the Trustees' accountant wrote Stephens on 29 March 1740, some five months before Stephens's visit to the unfinished guardhouse, to inquire how much "Noble Jones . . . [was paid] for building a watch house." [14] At any rate it is almost certain that the structure was completed by October 1740, when it was described as "a guard house built on a commodious place." [15] Perhaps Noble Jones built another

guardhouse elsewhere around Savannah, and it was this structure that the accountant was inquiring about earlier.

In the spring and first two months of the summer of 1740,
Jones accompanied Oglethorpe on his unsuccessful siege of
St. Augustine. It was probably immediately after their return
that Oglethorpe, fearing Spanish retaliation for their inva-
sion, became concerned with the defenses of the immediate
southern approach to Savannah, that is, Skidaway Narrows.
It was also probably at this time (August 1740) that Noble
Jones directed the construction (or at least the completion)
of the guardhouse on Pigeon Island.

The fort may well have been fashioned after the "Manchecolas" fort, St. Francis de Pupo in northern Florida, that
Jones had helped to capture a few weeks before on the Florida campaign. The Kimber term "Manchecolas" and the descriptions in 1741, "upon a piece of land which commands
the Narrows is a Timber Building, called Jones Fort" [16] and
"a Small Fort near his [Jones's] house," [17] seem to substan-
tiate this view. In any event, Jones did come to own the
island where DeBrahm shows the "Garde haus," acquiring
clear title to it by 1761. He later referred to the island in
his will as the "Island known by the name of the Redoubt," [18]
undoubtedly named for the fortification located there in the
1740s.

Apparently the guardhouse fell into ruin soon after the
1752 map was made. A later DeBrahm map (1757) of the
same area shows Jones's settlement using only a single "house"
symbol with no structures shown on Pigeon Island.

Available historical records do not contain other specific
descriptions of the plantation house or the guardhouse. However, one document suggests that Jones was constructing a
building in 1759–1760 (possibly at Wormslow) and another
document may be describing Wormslow as it appeared in
1765. In 1759–1760 Jones purchased thirteen pairs of hinges,
tools, at least five hundred nails, and two stock locks at

Thomas Rasberry's store in Savannah, which seems to indicate that he was doing some construction work.[19] And an entry in John Bartram's travels written in 1765 provides indirect evidence of the existence of Wormslow at that time. After Bartram visited Bethesda he "then rode to a gentleman's house which was delightfully situated on a large tide salt creek where ye oisters is as thich as they can be within a stone cast of his house." [20] It could be that the "gentleman's house" was Wormslow since it is located nearby, although Bartram does not specifically name the owner. However, he does go on to describe unusual fruit grown on the place (oranges, pomegranates, figs, peaches, apricots), and it is known that Noble Jones experimented with plants and trees. For example, an article in the *Georgia Gazette* of 1756 (the same year as Bartram's travels) stated: "Numbers of people from this place have gone . . . to the plantation of the Hon. Noble Jones, Esq. a few miles from town, to see an Agave plant, now in blossom there, which is said to be 27 and a half feet high." [21] Thus, Bartram may have been describing Wormslow when he stated: "[the people] generally builds piazas [on] one or more sides of thair houses which is commodious in these hot climates, they screen [off] ye scorching sunshine & draws ye breese finely & it must be extream hot indeed if one cant sit or walk comfortably in these when out of employ & much conversation both setting & walking is held in these." [22] It is unlikely that Bartram would have had to speculate on the discomfort of houses without piazzas if he had just finished visiting a house that had none. Therefore it is reasonable to conclude that if he had in fact visited Wormslow, then he had "conversed" on the porch. Bethesda has such a piazza on all four sides; hence, Bartram's experience with the type of house with the piazza on more than one side and perhaps his reference to a piazza on only one side were prompted by Jones's house.

In 1767 Noble Jones made his will leaving his "plantation

or tract of land containing five hundred acres known by the
Name of Wormslow . . . , household effects at Wormslow
and in Savannah . . . [and an] island known by the name of
the Redoubt containing 63 acres" to his unmarried daughter,
Mary. Noble Jones died in 1775 and was buried east of the
present tabby ruin site.[23]

MARY JONES'S OWNERSHIP
1775–1795

Whether Mary Jones, the new owner, actually lived at
Wormslow cannot be confirmed by historical records. However, since she acquired ownership of the place and also had
a house in town, it is reasonable to suppose that she divided
her time between her country and town houses. It is quite
probable that during the troubled years of the American
Revolution and the British occupation of Georgia, Mary
Jones lived in Savannah. In fact in September 1781 the
British advertised in the *Royal Georgia Gazette* that to satisfy
the "debt owed to the public" by Noble Jones, Wormslow
and two other tracts of Jones's land would be sold.[24] There is
no actual record of sale; perhaps the British never got around
to selling the property before their evacuation the next year.
Therefore it probably remained continuously in Mary Jones's
possession until her death in 1795. According to terms in
Noble Jones's will, the plantation then went to his son,
Noble Wimberly Jones.

A 1780 map indicates that Wormslow during Mary Jones's
ownership apparently was not a substantial working plantation (see fig. 4). The map simply shows a house and, to the
north, only a small section of cleared land, perhaps a garden
or a small cultivated field.[25]

NOBLE WIMBERLY JONES'S OWNERSHIP
1795–1804

Noble Wimberly Jones probably did not make Wormslow his home during his period of ownership since he already had an "ordinary house" on his plantation known as Lambeth (located nearby on the Little Ogeechee River) and several houses in Savannah.[26] He did, however, spend some time recovering from an illness at Wormslow in the fall of 1796, "to see what the change of air will do." [27] Wormslow did not remain in Noble Wimberly Jones's possession for long, however. When his son, George Jones, finished his education in 1804, Noble Wimberly Jones deeded the plantation to him.[28]

GEORGE JONES'S OWNERSHIP
1804–1837

George Jones, the grandson of Noble Jones, probably did not live at Wormslow at first. His principal working plantation was at nearby Poplar Grove, but he probably spent most of his time either in Savannah or at his home at Newton Plantation, at least until 1825.[29] During some of those years Jones had an overseer tending Wormslow. In 1810 he contracted John Rawls to "supervise and oversee" Wormslow for twelve months to raise cotton.[30] In 1819 Jones rented Wormslow to "Ann Reid, widow." The terms of the lease were as follows: "The building on his [Jones's] plantation called and known by the name of Wormslow together with twenty acres of land contiguous to said buildings . . . for the purposes of culture . . . and to make such repairs about the premises during the terms of this lease as may be necessary for the preservation of

Fig. 4. Detail of Campbell map of the Isle of Hope, 1780
(Georgia Department of Archives and History).

the buildings and her own convenience." [31] The description
in the lease can be interpreted to imply that there were only
twenty acres of cleared land at Wormslow at the time (much
as the Campbell map of 1780 implies) and that the buildings
were in something less than good repair. As for the location
of the main Wormslow buildings in the early nineteenth century, a map of Chatham County (see fig. 5) drawn in 1816
leaves little doubt that only the plantation building site was
located where the tabby ruins stand today. [32]

    In 1825, George Jones's country residence, Newton, burned
to the ground. After the fire Jones moved to Wormslow. [33] It

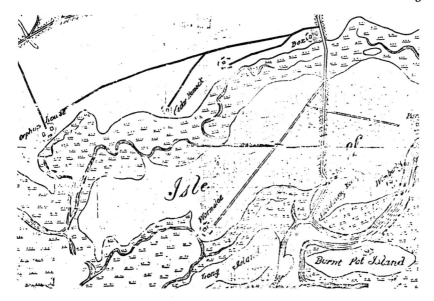

Fig. 5. Detail of McKinnon map of Chatham County, 1816
(S. Myrick Collection, Savannah, Ga.).

is logical to assume that because of the fire and his decision
to move to Wormslow permanently, George Jones decided to
abandon his grandfather's deteriorating tabby plantation on
the south point and build further up the Narrows, the site
of the present house at Wormsloe. On 25 July 1828 George
Jones entered into contract with Alexander J. C. Shaw "to
erect . . . a two story Timber and shingled building at
Wormsloe . . . 40′ × 20′ . . . on a basement of tabby or
brick . . . said building to be completed on or before the
first day of December next" [34] (see fig. 6). Thereafter Wormsloe became and remained the principal residence of the Jones
family and their descendants.

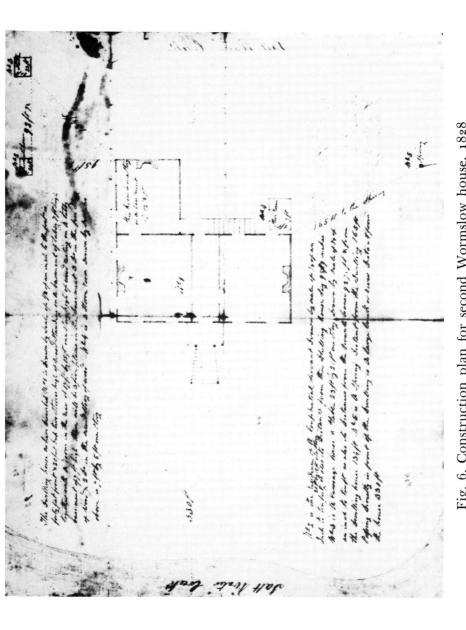

Fig. 6. Construction plan for second Wormslow house, 1828 (University of Georgia Libraries).

Archaeology

METHOD OF EXCAVATION

One of the primary objectives of the Wormslow excavation was to learn as much as possible about the tabby architecture. Therefore the digging was restricted to the area within and immediately adjacent to the existing ruins. The south central section of the ruins, thought to be the remains of the barracks, became the initial focus of the excavations, with the bastions of the enclosure wall and the wall itself following in that order. Since the digging was essentially part of the ruins preservation program, it was decided in the beginning that all of the in situ tabby remains had to be left undisturbed.

The excavations were organized and controlled by a grid system initially divided into fifty-foot squares (known as areas), each designated by a Roman numeral and a capital letter (see frontispiece). Each area in turn was divided into sixteen ten-foot squares, designated by Arabic numerals. Balks were left between the squares for stratification control points. Most of the excavation was done in areas IC and ID, and all of the squares and most of the balks were dug to natural undisturbed subsoil. One balk, running twenty-five feet north–south through the center of the remains of the building and east–west seventeen feet from the hearth to the center of the building was left unexcavated for any future excavation or rechecking of the stratigraphy.

Each square was assigned an excavation register number beginning with *1* and continuing consecutively through *33*, the last square opened. Lower case letters were in turn assigned to the various layers of stratigraphy. All topsoil layers were assigned the letter *a,* and the alphabetical sequence was continued until the natural subsoil was reached.

The digging took place during two concentrated time periods, October–December (total of twenty-one days) 1968, and 1 July–17 August 1969 (continuously). The trenches opened in 1968, ER 1–17, were left open until the following summer, at which time they were finished along with the additional trenches ER 18–33. A total of eighteen people intermittently helped with the excavation either as full-time paid workers or as volunteers. The regular excavation staff consisted primarily of six people.

Before the second excavation period (summer 1969), a full probe test to a depth of three feet was conducted at one-foot intervals across the entire area enclosed by the tabby wall. With the exception of two layers, later found to be a trash pit and the brick well, no additional major disturbances or masonry remains were detected. Intermittent probing to the same depth outside the tabby ruins indicated no other masonry within fifty feet of the tabby ruins.

During the week beginning 23 August 1969 the site was filled back to the previous modern grade with the excavation spoil. However, the southeast corner of the building ruins was left uncovered for future stabilization and the well area was left open for repair work.

SUMMARY CONCLUSIONS

The archaeological excavations (see figs. 7 and 8) revealed that Wormslow had been occupied from about the 1730s to the first quarter of the nineteenth century, and the remains of a building (the main plantation house) surrounded by a tabby enclosure wall in the shape of a four-bastioned fort were found. More specifically evidence was found indicating:

Fig. 7. Archaeological excavations at Wormslow, looking south, 1969.

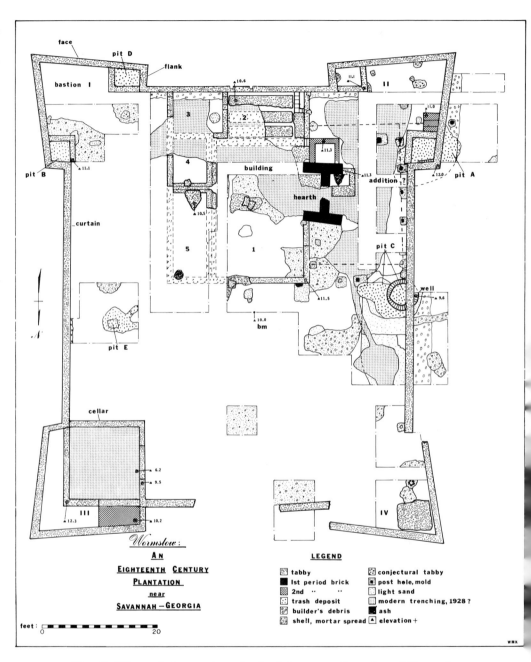

Fig. 8. Plan of the archaeological features found at Wormslow,
1968–1969.

(1) an early occupation period (ca. 1737–1740) predating the tabby work, within which a trash pit was filled (pit A), a brick well constructed, and possibly a wattle and daub hut built; (2) a tabby construction period (ca. 1739–1744), probably of long duration, within which the house, an outbuilding, and fort wall were constructed; (3) possibly an additional construction period (ca. 1750–1770), in which the house was expanded; (4) a period when the well was abandoned and backfilled with domestic trash (ca. 1770–1790) (pit C); (5) a final occupation period (ca. 1800–1820), indicated primarily by another trash pit. Two additional accumulations of trash (pit B and pit D) were deposited at the site during the eighteenth century, probably in the periods 1750–1760 and 1785–? respectively. In addition to the events of the eighteenth and early nineteenth centuries, archaeological evidence suggests that there had been a period when a considerable portion of the tabby work had been razed and removed from the site, and in the present century several trenches had been dug across the ruins (probably by Marmaduke Floyd in 1928), considerably disturbing the occupation levels.

EARLY OCCUPATION

Pit A

A domestic refuse pit (pit A) located in the southwest corner of the ruins under a portion of bastion II and a brick well located partially under the west tabby fort wall were the earliest features found at the site. Their position under the tabby work shows that they predate the tabby construction period, and the existence of the pit filled with trash indicates that there was definitely a pretabby period of occupation at the site. Moreover, pieces of what appear to be mortar from wattle and daub construction were found under the tabby footings of the house, further evidence of occupation at the site before the tabby structures were built. However, no structural evidence relating to the earliest period was found.

Pit A amounted merely to an irregular hole 10′ × 12′ dug originally to a depth of 3′ into the natural subsoil. In the hole, wood ash, garbage, and trash were deposited until the cavity was completely backfilled (see figs. 9 and 10). It appears that the western side of the pit then became a "trash heap" and that the resulting mound had to be leveled again during the construction of the fort wall (discussed below). Because the heavy tabby construction was subsequently built over the loose trash filling in the pit, the wall later began to sag, necessitating a brick underpinning operation (see fig. 11). During repair some of the earlier trash became mixed with the upper level of fill.

Most of the fill in pit A consisted of animal bones and wood ash, but a few sherds of pottery and ten broken wine bottles were also found. Three of the wine bottles could be mended,

Fig. 9. East–west cross section through pit A.

and enough remained of the others to show that at least three types of wine bottles were present: a broad-based, short-necked style predominantly manufactured in the period 1730–1745; a similar but more cylindrical style of the period 1735–1750; and the predominant type (six examples), a short cylindrical style with slightly concave walls, of the period 1735–1760.[1] The pottery was made in the same general period. Fragments of lead-glazed coarse earthenware, white-

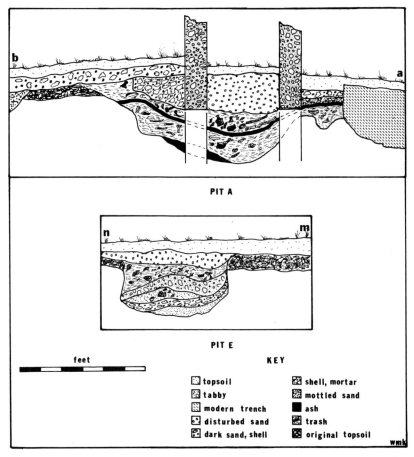

PIT A

PIT E

feet   KEY

🗒 topsoil   🔳 shell, mortar
🔳 tabby   🔳 mottled sand
🔳 modern trench   ■ ash
🔳 disturbed sand   🔳 trash
🔳 dark sand, shell   🔳 original topsoil

wmk

Fig. 10. East–west cross section through pit A and pit E
(see frontispiece, line a–b and line m–n).

glazed delftware hand painted in blue, drab white saltglazed stoneware, and a fragment of chocolate-glazed red stoneware can all be dated to the second quarter of the eighteenth century, although all of these types continued to be made and used later. It would be reasonably safe to say, however, that the combined evidence of the wine bottles and the pottery points to a deposition in the period 1735–1760.

The historical evidence combined with the archaeological data can narrow the deposition date of pit A more precisely. The DeBrahm map of 1752 leaves little doubt that the tabby fort wall existed by that date, and records mark the beginning of Jones's occupation of the site in 1737. Since the wall was built over the pit and since Noble Jones was apparently the first to occupy the site, it follows that the pit was filled in

Fig. 11. Brick repair in bastion II.

the period 1737–1752. Moreover, the general description of
"Mr. Jones' " plantation made in February 1741 seems to imply that the tabby work was well under way by that date;
therefore any pretabby occupation (i.e., the filling of pit A)
must have taken place in the period 1737–1740.

Well Construction

The brick well located near the middle of the west curtain
also predates the tabby construction since the wall had been
built over it (see fig. 18). The well was not abandoned because of the tabby construction. Marks along the wall base
show that a wooden "box" was constructed to bridge the well
opening, which enabled the wall to be built without backfilling the shaft. The shaft itself measures 3'6" in diameter,
is 9'3" deep and was constructed with wedge-shaped "well
bricks" or compass bricks 8½" × 5" × 3", 2⅜" thick. For
some unexplained reason, one course of rectangular bricks
(8½" × 4" × 2⅜") laid on edge had been used 3'6" down
from the top. A 10' × 10' hole filled with mixed light sand
was found to have been dug and backfilled completely around
the brick shaft. This feature probably represents the backfilled builder's trench for the well construction and was probably dug down to the eighteenth-century water table. From
that point, apparently the well had been built from the top
down, whereby the bricks were laid from above the water
table on a wooden ring, then lowered the remaining three
feet by undercutting. The wooden ring used in the construction was found intact at the base of the bricks. (The subsequent collapse and backfilling of the well shaft will be discussed below.)

The only artifacts found in the backfilling in the builder's
trench around the well were four undatable nails and a
minute sherd of yellow-glazed slipware, a type made throughout the late seventeenth and eighteenth centuries. Therefore
the only dating clues for the well construction were its posi-

tion in relation to the tabby wall and, consequently, its association with pit A. Since the wall overlies both pit A and
the well, and since historical and archaeological evidence
point to a deposition date of 1737–1740 for pit A and the construction of the tabby wall, it follows that the well had been
built in the same early occupation period.

Wattle and Daub Construction

No other major features were found predating the tabby construction, but it is hardly logical that the occupants would
have constructed a well and occupied the site long enough to
dig and fill a trash pit without building some type of dwelling. A possible clue to the dwelling can be supplied by one
isolated bit of archaeological evidence and, again, the historical record. Fragments of mortar or thick plaster with impressions of what appear to be wattling on one side were found
packed beneath one of the tabby footings of the house, and
more examples were found scattered across the site (see fig.
45). (The plaster found in association with the destruction
of the tabby house [discussed below] shows that it had been
laid on regular lathing.) It was the usual practice in Georgia
to build "thatched bowers" or wattle and mortar daub "huts"
to live in until more permanent structures could be erected
(see chapter 3). No definite outlines of such huts were found
inside the excavation area at Wormslow, yet it is not beyond
the realm of possibility that Jones first erected such a wattle
and daub structure, built his well (the only fresh water supply anywhere near the site), and deposited his trash in pit A
while he was first clearing the land. Moreover, both Jones
and his workmen needed some type of shelter to use during
the tabby construction and a fresh water supply (one of the
primary necessities for the work). Probing to the west of the
pit and well, outside the present tabby ruins, failed to show
any evidence of huts, but there is little reason to expect that
such temporary shelters would leave more than postholes or

soil stains. Huts still existed by 1744, when it was stated that the marines under Jones's command lived in huts near his house. Whether these huts date back to the original occupation period at the site is not certain, but it is reasonably safe to say from the archaeological evidence that their existence during the first period of occupation is at least a distinct possibility.

THE TABBY HOUSE

House Plan

Considerable evidence of the tabby period of occupation was found during the course of the excavations; sections of the house foundations, partitions, chimney base, and floors were found (see figs. 12 and 13). The foundations of the house were built on a north–south axis with the outside dimensions measuring 32'6" × 24' and with the wall footing itself measuring between 1' and 1'6" thick. The house had at least five rooms: room 1 (15' × 22') in the northwest corner; room 2 (13' × 7'6") in the southwest corner; and three smaller rooms, rooms 3, 4, and 5 (7' × 8', 6'6" × 8' and 6'6" × 14'), along the east wall. Evidence for four, and possibly five, doorways was found; one at the center of the south wall, one opposite to it on the north wall, and three along the west wall. The doorway at the center of the south wall and the doorway in the southwest corner had 4" × 4" slots in the tabby on each side of the passageway, and the doorway north of the chimney had one 4" × 4" slot. Postholes were found beneath each slot and a similar posthole was found in line with the remaining section of the north wall footing, suggesting that a doorway was located at the center of this wall also. The house apparently had one other doorway, just south of the chimney base. It was the narrowest of all, and the south jamb had been partially filled with brick.

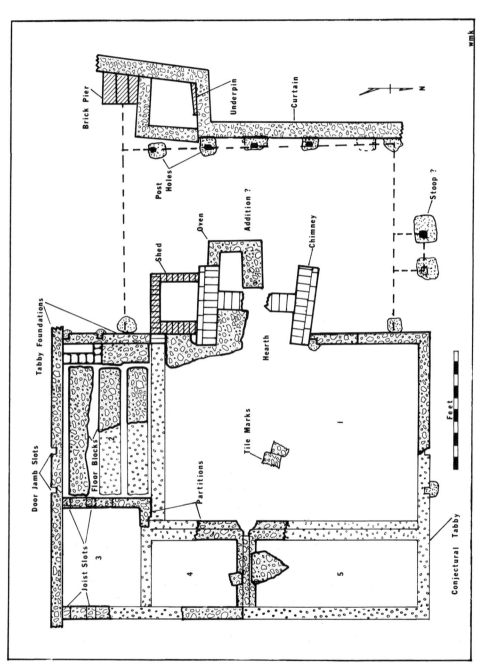

Fig. 12. Detail plan of the house at Wormslow.

Fig. 13. Tabby partitions and floor fragments (center) in house at Wormslow.

Chimney Base

The west wall footing of the house had been built onto a large H-shaped brick chimney base laid in English bond. The foundation measures 6′6″ × 10′ overall with a 6′6″ × 3′ hearth on the inside and a 6′6″ × 2′6″ hearth on the outside. The chimney is located on the long axis of the house, is 1′3″ off center, and is slightly turned at an angle to the wall. In fact the chimney legs are not exactly parallel, with the north leg being as much as 6″ out of line. The legs are about 1′6″ wide. Nine courses still remain of the entire foundation, with the exception of the central section of the hearth, which apparently had been disturbed by modern trenching. One section of the hearth remained relatively undisturbed, the south half of the interior, and in it a small section of the thin tabby fire palate still remained intact. A small tabby and brick footing was found in the south half of the outside hearth, presumably the remains of an oven. Also a small brick footing measuring 5' × 4' was added to the south side of the chimney base on the outside, immediately in front of the narrowest doorway on the west wall.

Floors and Partitions

Although the interior of the house had been severely disturbed by root action, the apparent razing of the structure, and the trenches of the 1920s, some evidence of the floors in the rooms still remained reasonably undisturbed. In room 2, two relatively whole and two broken sections of the original tabby floor were uncovered along with the brickbat foundation for a step in front of the southwest doorway. The floor had been laid in three 2' × 11' × 3" and one 1'6" × 4' rectangular blocks. Each of the blocks had 4" gaps between them, probably once having contained the wooden form boards. Small sections of tabby flooring were also found in room 4 and room 5, apparently having been protected from the 1928 trenching by roots of the large cedar tree which has grown up inside the northeast corner of the ruins. The tabby floors in these rooms had been constructed in long narrow blocks, similar to those uncovered in room 2. Impressions in the tabby partition footing (apparently caused by a 4" × 4" wooden sill laid on the wet tabby) between rooms 4 and 5, and the neat squared-off ends of both floor-block fragments show that the floor was poured in flush with the existing partition sills. A similar sill impression shows on the partition footing separating room 4 and room 5 from room 1 (see fig. 12). In addition a 4" × 4" slot through the tabby suggests the location of the wooden corner post for the partition wall between rooms 4 and 5.

The narrow tabby partition footing separating the two south rooms of the house (rooms 2 and 3) also shows some evidence of sill impressions. Moreover, impressions, but of a different nature, were found in the east exterior wall and the west partition of room 3. These marks were 9″ across and spaced 1′6″ apart, probably indicating the size and spacing of wooden floor joists. It follows therefore that, unlike the other rooms of the house, room 3 had had an elevated wooden floor.

The floor in the largest room of the house, presumably the original kitchen (room 1), had been extremely disturbed by later digging. However, two rectangular impressions in the soft mortar subfloor were found in the center of the room, indicating that perhaps the kitchen had once had a brick tile floor. No tiles were found in place, but two corner fragments from brick tiles were found elsewhere on the site, serving as indirect evidence for the kitchen flooring. All that was left undisturbed in the remaining part of room 1 were scattered sections of the yellow sand subfloor.

Stratigraphy

The stratification in and around the house was relatively uncomplicated, at least in the areas where the eighteenth-century occupation levels remained undisturbed. In the south end of the house (left relatively undisturbed by later trenching) (see fig. 14) the soil levels consisted of: (1) a 6″ layer of dark mottled sand (the original topsoil); above that (2) a thin spread of fine gray mortar, probably laid down during the tabby construction or wall plastering; (3) 1′ of yellow sand, apparently deposited to act as a level subfloor for the wood, tabby or tile floors in the rooms; (4) the floor itself; and finally, (5) 3″ of topsoil.

The stratification of the fire palate (see fig. 15) consisted of a thin layer of fine tabby or mortar overlying 6″ of light gray mortar dust which in turn covered 1′6″ of burnt orange

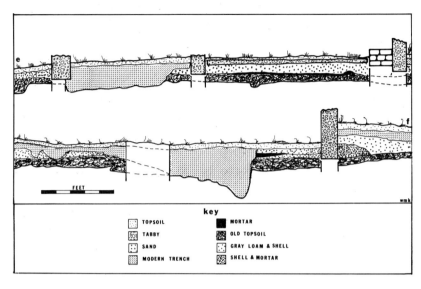

key

▦	TOPSOIL	▓	MORTAR
▦	TABBY	▦	OLD TOPSOIL
▦	SAND	▦	GRAY LOAM & SHELL
▦	MODERN TRENCH	▦	SHELL & MORTAR

Fig. 14. East–west cross section through the house and the west tabby enclosure wall (bastion II) (see frontispiece, line e–f).

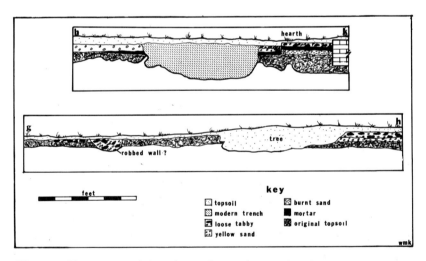

key

▦	topsoil	▦	burnt sand
▦	modern trench	▪	mortar
▦	loose tabby	▦	original topsoil
▦	yellow sand		

Fig. 15. East–west (above) and north–south (below) cross sections through kitchen (room 1) (see frontispiece line h–k and line g–h).

and mottled dark sand. The sand probably represents the backfilling of the builder's trench dug during the construction of the chimney, although no clear edge to the trench itself was discernible. The mortar dust level above the sand was presumably part of the mortar spread associated with the construction and/or plastering of the house. There was also some indication in the cross section that a 4″ × 4″ timber had been placed along the edge of the hearth between the tabby fire palate and the tile floor.

The north half of the interior of the house had been extremely disturbed in the years since occupation, having been dug out as much as 1′ below the level of the south interior rooms (see fig. 15). This disturbance probably occurred during the trenching of the 1920s, but no clear-cut trench lines were found. The soil levels encountered in this area of the house consisted merely of the present topsoil overlying the dark original topsoil, except in the extreme northwest and northeast corners of room 1. In the northwest corner some of the mortar level associated with tabby construction remained intact, and in the northeast corner some concentration of oyster shell was found in line with the north wall of the house, perhaps representing a robbed wall slot. Finally, tree root action had disturbed some of the stratigraphy in rooms 1, 4, and 5. Apparently the same cedar tree roots that had protected the sections of tabby flooring in rooms 4 and 5 had disturbed approximately 7′ of the occupation levels near the center of the house, rendering the reading of the stratification in this area impossible.

As the digging progressed into the construction debris levels associated with the house, it became increasingly clear that no precise builder's trenches had been used in the construction of the walls; that is, the walls were laid directly on the old topsoil. However, a layer of light gray sandy loam with bits of charcoal and shell (much like the fine mortar layer inside the house but not as compact) was found adjacent to

the undisturbed areas next to the three walls at the south end
of the house. Wherever this level was found throughout the
site, it extended to the tabby walls but never under them. In
all probability, therefore, this level represents lime, mortar,
and tabby spillover deposited during the tabby construction
period.

Dating

Very few artifacts were found in the construction levels associated with the house. However, the ceramics that were
recovered are the earliest types found at the site. The bases
from two delftware vessels, a pale blue ointment-pot base and
a pinkish white drug jar base (see fig. 47, nos. 11 and 12)
were found in the yellow sand fill beneath the floors in rooms
2 and 3. Although not tightly datable, both vessels could well
have been made in the late seventeenth or first half of the
eighteenth century. One clay tobacco pipe stem was also recovered in the sand beneath a tabby floor block in room 2.
Its stem hole diameter, $\frac{5}{64}''$, is by no means conclusive dating
evidence, but, with little else to go on, it can be used as additional evidence for a deposition date in the first half of the
1700s. One other delft ointment-pot base (fig. 47, no. 13)
was recovered during the course of the excavations in a level
that was also apparently deposited during the construction of
the house. The sherd was found in a layer of light gray loam
with bits of shell deposited along the interior of the south
fort wall, just outside the southwest doorway to the house.
Since the central section of the south fort wall also served as
the south wall of the house, the sherd was probably deposited
at the same time that the house itself was constructed. The
base is also of the same body and glaze as the ointment-pot
found in the house fill, and therefore it too could date from
the first half of the eighteenth century.

Several fragments of unglazed coarse earthenware were
also recovered along the south fort wall in the same construc-

tion level (and elsewhere on the site in construction levels) but are largely undatable (see fig. 46, nos. 13 and 14). However, the presence of earthenware, primarily in construction levels, aided in the recognition of construction debris when soil color was absent. The recovery of four small sherds of a flared rim, waisted white saltglazed stoneware cup in two levels presumed to have been deposited during construction aided in more precise archaeological dating: two were found in the light gray loam and shell levels along the exterior of the west house wall and two were in the backfilling of the interior of the east hearth. The sherds could not be cross-mended, but the color and shape suggest that they came from the same vessel and were deposited at about the same time. This type of saltglazed stoneware has been found on other sites in an archaeological context of 1729 and was generally manufactured in the period circa 1720–1740.[2] Thus the combined ceramic evidence points to a construction period after 1720 and probably before 1750.

One other artifact provides more definite dating evidence. The neck from a glass wine bottle of a style manufactured in the period 1730–1745 was found actually sealed in the base of the tabby partition footing separating rooms 4 and 5. (See fig. 16 and fig. 50, no. 11). It was without question deposited just before or during the tabby construction and therefore adds considerable weight to the contention that the tabby construction took place in the second quarter of the eighteenth century.

Once again by turning to the historical record and combining it with the archaeological evidence, a more precise date for the tabby construction can be postulated. As mentioned above, the tabby fort and probably the house were completed by 1752, and the description of Wormslow written in 1744 suggests that the house and fort were completed by that date. The only other description (1741) clearly states that the house was in the process of being built (probably nearing

Fig. 16. Bottle neck of 1730–1745 style in situ beneath partition base of house.

completion) in that year. However, it should be pointed out that tabby construction is a slow process requiring a considerable labor force, which Noble Jones would not have had until 1750, when slaves were allowed in the colony. But after late 1739 or early 1740 the ten marines under his command would have been available to do the work. Therefore, since the artifacts found in association with construction seem to point to the period circa 1735–1745, the years indicated by the historical records, 1739–1744, seem to be the most likely time in which the house (and probably the whole tabby complex of structures) was built.

The small brickbat foundation, probably the base for a woodshed next to the chimney foundation, appears to have been added sometime after 1744. It was built on the tabby construction debris level next to the west wall, but no datable artifacts were found in association with it. The tabby and brick oven base in the west hearth could have been constructed at the same time or later when an outshut kitchen was probably added to the west side of the house.

The Addition

A small brick pier (see fig. 17) located in bastion II, a series of postholes along the west fort wall, and two postholes along the west wall of the house seem to indicate that a frame shed or outshut was added to the house sometime after the original tabby construction (see fig. 12). The brick pier had obviously supported a heavy load (such as a large wooden sill) for three of its central courses had been pushed down into the subsoil. It is likely that the pier supported the southwest corner of the addition, although no evidence of a similar pier was found at what should have been the northwest corner. The addition would have measured 16' × 23', and there is some evidence to indicate that the north corner of the bastion had been included inside the additional room or rooms. The west hearth of the main chimney would have then been included inside the addition, and perhaps this hearth had been originally built in the chimney with the future addition in mind. Two postholes were also found to the north of the addition, perhaps marking the location of the doorway and front stoop.

Most of the archaeological evidence for the addition had been destroyed by the widest and deepest of the 1928 trenches, but most of the postholes and the one brick pier were left relatively undisturbed. In all cases where the upper levels had been left untouched, the postholes cut through the tabby construction level. Moreover, the brick pier was built on the construction debris and upon an additional occupation accumulation. Therefore it would be reasonable to conclude that the addition not only followed the tabby construction in chronological sequence, but probably a considerable length of time elapsed after the tabby work before the outshut was built. Unfortunately the post-molds and the occupation level under the brick pier were relatively free of datable artifacts, containing only nails and bits of brick. However, the posthole in the south end of trench 16 contained a small fragment of a white delft drug jar base banded in blue, which was probably manufactured in the early eighteenth century, and the posthole at the southeast corner of the addition contained plain white saltglazed stoneware fragments, a type probably made in the second or third quarter of the eighteenth century. Thus from this evidence and the fact that the postholes cut through the tabby construction debris, it could be concluded that the addition was built in the period circa 1744–1775.

The association of one of the postholes of the addition, the west posthole for the stoop, along with another more datable archaeological feature of the site, the trash deposit next to the well (pit C) , and the indirect historical evidence

Fig. 17. Brick pier support for probable addition to the house, showing construction and occupation layers beneath.

do not refute the 1744–1775 date for the addition. In fact it can be interpreted in such a way as to suggest a more precise date. The west posthole is partially covered by trash pit C (see fig. 8), next to the well, which was deposited after 1770 (see below). It therefore follows logically that the addition was built after 1744, the date of the completion of the tabby work, and before 1770, the earliest date for the filling of the trash pit near the well. Also, the bills of Noble Jones from Rasberry's store dated 1759 and 1760 show that he had purchased a considerable amount of building hardware, hinges, nails, and door locks, which could have been intended for the construction of the addition at Wormslow. Therefore the actual construction date for the addition may well have been 1759 or 1760.

THE WELL ABANDONMENT AND PIT C

Excavations around and in the abandoned brick well (see figs. 18–20) along the west curtain revealed that it had probably been used for a considerable time after the tabby construction and that the east wall, weakened from constant use, had partially collapsed causing erosion and a cave-in to occur next to it. Subsequently both the washed-out cavity and the well shaft were used for trash disposal.

Stratification

The major levels encountered in the excavation of the well in their probable order of deposition were: (1) 10′ × 10′ hole filled with mixed light sand, the builder's trench (discussed above); (2) clean sandy wash and a pile of bricks from the collapse of the wall at the bottom of the shaft; (3) more sand wash tipping in from the cave-in into the east side of the shaft; (4) a deposit of domestic trash in the caved-in hole, spilling into the interior of the shaft through the break in the wall; (5) five feet of domestic trash filling the remaining section of the well shaft and the upper foot of the caved-in hole; (6) a narrow modern search trench (1928?) cutting through part of the east edge of the exterior trash pit; and, (7) a 4″ to 6″ layer of topsoil. Outside the curtain wall the sequence of soil levels was exactly the same as it was elsewhere along the outside of the tabby wall. A gray mortar and shell level had accumulated, probably during construction, next to the tabby wall, above the old topsoil; and above that a layer of brown loam and shell had built up during the occupation period.

The position of the well beneath the tabby curtain wall shows that it had been built during the earliest occupation period at the site (shown above to have occurred during the period 1737–1741). However, no datable artifacts were found at the bottom to indicate how long the well was used. But as the digging progressed into the shaft, it became increasingly more obvious that the bricks along the eastern side of the

Fig. 18. Detail of well showing east–west cross section through the builder's trench and pit C.

Fig. 19. Well interior showing trash
in situ (pit C).

shaft had been worn into a concave groove by constant fric-
tion of the bucket against the edge. Of course it could not be
determined exactly how long it would take to wear such a
groove, but it is likely that the wearing away process must
have taken a number of years. In fact it was apparently the
wear itself that eventually led to the partial collapse and subsequent abandonment of the well.

Dating

The deposit of trash in the caved-in hole and the upper six
feet of the well shaft turned out to be a virtual archaeological
gold mine, providing both valuable cultural information

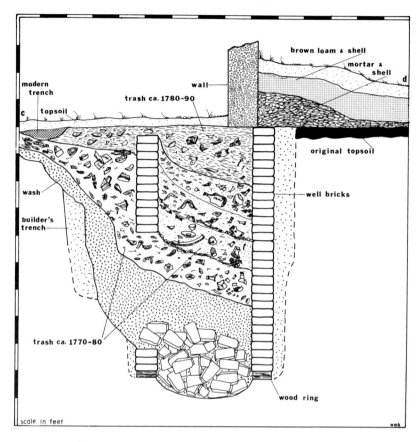

Fig. 20. East–west cross section through well
(see frontispiece, line c–d).

concerning the middle years of occupation at the site and
dating evidence for the use of the well. The stratigraphy
suggests two, and possibly three, separate deposition periods
(fig. 20): (1) the initial filling of the cave-in and the lower
1′4″ of the trash in the well shaft; (2) the deposition of the
next 3′ of trash in the well shaft; and (3) the filling of the
remaining sections of the shaft and the caved-in hole. At least
twelve different ceramic types were found in the three deposits, ranging from delftware to creamware and pearlware,

the latter confined to level 3 and the creamware to levels 2 and 3. Since the presence of creamware in the other colonies in America seems to be datable to after 1769, and since pearlware apparently did not arrive in America before 1785 (at least in Virginia), it is very tempting to assign a three-stage chronological buildup of the materials beginning in the late 1760s and taking place over a number of years.[3] Moreover, there were at least 127 vessels deposited in all, and it is hardly likely, short of an earthquake, that that many vessels could be accidently broken and thrown away in a short period of time. Also, scratch blue, white saltglazed stoneware was the latest ceramic type recovered in level 1, a type datable to the third quarter of the eighteenth century and usually found elsewhere in this country on sites occupied in the 1770s (see fig. 48, nos. 3 and 4). Therefore it would at least be reasonable to conclude from ceramic evidence alone that levels 1 and 2 were deposited throughout the period circa 1770–1780, and that level 3 was added after 1785. And there is every reason to believe that the entire trash pit was deposited in the general period 1770–1790.

At least twenty-five wine bottles were thrown into the well (pit C), the latest style recovered in both levels 1 and 2 being a type manufactured in the period 1770–1800 (see fig. 50, no. 7). Other generally datable glassware items included a wineglass stem, probably manufactured in the period 1745–1760 (level 1), fragments of an engraved drinking glass or "rummer" made in the period 1760–1820, fragments from a Turlington's BALSOM OF LIFE medicine bottle (post-1754), and a pharmaceutical bottle base typical of the period 1760–1780 (see fig. 51, nos. 1, 4, 9, and 13).

Twenty-nine clay tobacco pipe stems were also found in pit C. Using J. C. Harrington's system of dating by stem hole diameter, the samples produced a mid-eighteenth-century date.[4] The Lewis Binford formula yielded a date of about 1760, but it should be pointed out that if the deposits

date as late as the ceramics and bottles suggest, then the
pipe stem dating evidence would have to be looked upon with
caution. Moreover, twenty-nine samples are hardly enough
to produce a reliable date for any deposit.[5]

There may be some relationship between the levels of trash
fill in the well and the recorded events at Wormslow in the
1770s and 1780s. The two earliest levels of trash may well
have been deposited during the last few years of Noble Jones's
occupation of the site, the bulk of the tools and early ceramics
having been found at these levels. Upon Jones's death in
1775 Wormslow went to his daughter, Mary, who probably
remained in Savannah during the British occupation and the
troubled times of the Revolution, leaving Wormslow abandoned. After the war it is likely that Mary Jones returned to
the plantation. Thus the final level of trash, containing the
latest ceramic style, pearlware, could well be the remnants of
the later occupation and could explain the apparent halt and
subsequent completion of the backfilling of the well.

Some evidence of the existence of a later well was found
during the excavations (fig. 8). However, this feature was
all but completely obliterated by the excavations of the
1920s. Approximately 10′ north of the brick well, a round
hole about 7″ in diameter was found. Like the nearby brick
well, this feature had a roughly rectangular hole around it
(the builder's trench?) filled with mixed white and yellow
sand. However, this builder's trench did not go under the
tabby fort wall, perhaps indicating that it had been constructed after the tabby construction period. No datable artifacts were found in the backfilling, but it is reasonable to
assume that it had been built after the brick well collapsed
circa 1770–1780. Apparently the second well shaft had been
encountered by a narrow search trench of the 1928 excavation, then completely excavated. The only dating evidence
provided by the re-excavation of the feature was a pine stake
found in the mixed fill, proving that recent digging had taken
place there. However, no parts of the well were found in

situ; therefore even the identification of the "hole" as a well is no more than a logical possibility.

TABBY FORTIFICATION

The fort wall was the most complete standing feature of the Wormslow ruins. The footings for the entire enclosure, in some places standing 8' high, were plainly visible before excavations began. Therefore a more thorough architectural study of the aboveground ruins is presented below. It was the task of the archaeologist to look for builder's trenches and other construction levels to use for dating evidence and to learn as much as possible about the method of construction itself. Only selected trenches were made at given locations along the walls and inside the bastions, particularly bastions I and II. The small tabby footings inside the south bastions were also excavated because of the possibility that the fill within them was deposited at the time of construction.

Stratification

Layers of gray loam and shell, the same composition as the levels associated with the construction of the house, were found adjacent to the tabby walls. Once again no "builder's trench" as such was found, the walls having been laid directly on the original topsoil. Because there was no trench to follow, it was extremely difficult to decide what material was directly mixed in with the builder's debris and what had merely fallen next to the wall due to subsequent occupation and erosion. However, in most cases the construction debris appeared to be more concentrated and compact than the later levels.

Dating

There is every reason to believe that nearly all of the major tabby work on the site was built at the same time as the house,

circa 1740–1744. It was pointed out above that the south
curtain served as the south wall of the house and that the
west wall was built over pit A and the well, and that historical records indicate that the construction took place in the
late 1730s or early 1740s. The artifacts found in the construction levels of the curtain wall and the bastions do not
refute any of this dating evidence. Numerous varieties of undatable coarse earthenware and slipware were found in the
construction debris, and only one sherd of more datable pottery, a fragment of a delft plate decorated with a chinoiserie
crosshatched border design, could be dated more specifically
than eighteenth century (i.e., ca. 1730–1760).[6] One wine
bottle neck was found with the delftware. It had apparently
come from a type of bottle manufactured in the period 1735–
1760. Therefore archaeologically it can be safely stated only
that the walls and bastions were constructed after the well
and the deposition of the trash in pit A and probably at the
same time as the house.

PIT B

The excavation of the 4'6" × 4'6" tabby foundation in the
north flank of bastion I showed that it had been backfilled
with trash (pit B). The bulk of the artifacts was confined to
the upper 1'6" of fill which lay above a dark brown sand
level containing oyster shells and a few animal bones. The
lowest level probably had been deposited during construction, with the trash deposit occurring later after the tabby
foundation was no longer needed as a part of the defense
system.

The trash in pit B was predominantly made up of bottle
glass. Fragments of at least sixty-eight wine bottles and four
case bottles were found, the latest and predominant type
dating in the period 1735–1760 (see fig. 50, nos. 8, 9, 10, 12,

13, 20, and 21). The datable ceramics consisted of a rim sherd from a molded white saltglazed stoneware plate dating after 1740 (see fig. 48, no. 9) and fragments from a small dry-body red stoneware teapot decorated in small sprig molded animal and floral designs (see fig. 49, no. 7). Such vessels are commonly found on colonial sites of the third quarter of the eighteenth century. Therefore, combining the ceramic and glass evidence, the trash in pit B was probably deposited in the period circa 1750–1760.

PIT D

Two other concentrations of artifacts were found in the course of the excavations. Both included evidence of the later period of occupation at the site. Pit D, located within the small tabby footing in the south flank of bastion I, contained an upper layer of brickbats, some soot covered on one edge. Bricks used in chimney flues usually become soot covered in this manner. Of course the brickbats themselves are undatable, but they are the same general color and size as the bricks used in the chimney base of the house. Perhaps the brickbats were discarded when the chimney was dismantled, the unbroken bricks salvaged for later construction elsewhere. Below the bricks a layer of dark gray loam with bits of charcoal and oyster shell was found. Finally a spread of light gray loam and shell was found associated with the base of the tabby work, the same type of layer shown above to have been deposited during the tabby construction. All of the artifacts, with the exception of some undatable bottle glass, came from the second level.

The artifacts found in the level below the brickbats can give the destruction and abandonment period at the site a general *terminus post quem* date. Although the deposit contained the rim from a light blue delft mug of about mid-eighteenth-century manufacture (see fig. 46, no. 8), it also contained a molded "dot, diaper, and basket" patterned white saltglazed stoneware plate (ca. 1740–1780), a light cream-ware plate in the royal pattern (probably made after 1785), and a neck from a bottle style made primarily in the last quarter of the eighteenth century (see fig. 48, nos. 9 and 13; and fig. 50, no. 15). Therefore it can be safely stated that the trash in pit D was deposited after 1785 and that the chimney (and probably the other masonry structures) were disman-tled and abandoned sometime after that.

PIT E

The other concentration of trash, pit E, located about 8′ from the middle of the east curtain, proved to be more helpful in determining the full extent of the occupation period at the site. The pit consisted of a slightly oval hole (4′ × 6′) dug to a depth of 3′ 6″. The lower 2′ of fill in the pit contained "piles" of decomposed tabby, perhaps surplus material left over from later repairs (see fig. 10). The presence of a mortar and brickbat plug (see fig. 45) (similar to those used on the nearby curtain to backfill holes in the tabby left by the form pegs) and a sherd of prehistoric Indian pottery coated with tabby (a similar type was found imbedded in the nearby wall) suggest that the pit was dug originally for the disposal of leftover repair materials. After the tabby was discarded, a layer of light gray loam with wood ash and domestic trash was deposited in the pit.

At least thirty-four fragmented ceramic vessels were found in the upper level of pit E, and at least twelve of the vessels were made of pearlware. Most of the pearlware was either hand painted in blue or banded in brown, but one sherd had been decorated with a blue transfer-printed design, a tech-nique used on pearlware no earlier than 1787 and popular

INCHES

Fig. 21. Trash in situ, pit E.

primarily in the period 1790–1820. Since no later artifacts were found in the pit (and indeed throughout the digging on the rest of the site), it would be reasonable to conclude that pit E was dug and filled during the last years of occupation at the site, circa 1790–1820. Moreover, it logically follows that the abandonment of the site occurred sometime toward the end of that period and that the partial dismantling of the masonry features occurred soon after.

Historical records can help define the terminal occupation period more precisely. It was pointed out above that John Rawls entered into contract with George Jones to serve as overseer for Wormslow in 1810, and in 1819 Ann Reid became a tenant at Wormslow. It is almost certain therefore that occupation continued at the site in the second decade of the nineteenth century. Moreover there is a possibility that the 1819 lease explains the purpose of pit E. Under the terms of the lease Ann Reid was required to "make such repairs about the premises . . . as may be necessary for the preservation of the buildings and her own convenience."[7] It may be that the evidence of the late repairing found in pit E was actually the result of the implementation of the terms of the lease by Mrs. Reid.

A comparison of the ceramic types and number of vessels in the well fill (pit C, all levels) with the artifacts from pit E gives more exact evidence for the contention that the fill in pit E was in fact deposited later (see fig. 22). The presence of pearlware in both deposits merely gives the *terminus post quem* date of 1785–1790. Even though transfer-printed pearlware was found in pit E and not pit C, that fact alone is not unquestionable evidence that pit E was filled later. But it is extremely probable that after the introduction of pearlware to America, circa 1785, earlier ceramic types began to disappear, being replaced gradually by more popular wares, creamware and pearlware. There is the possibility therefore that a trash deposit of about 1785 would contain a greater

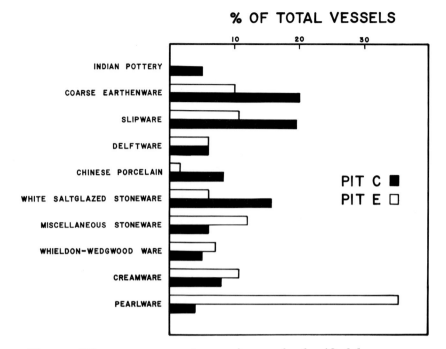

Fig. 22. The percentage of ceramic vessels classified by ware recovered in pit C and pit E.

percentage of vessels (not sherds) of earlier manufacture date than a deposit made around 1800. A vessel count made for pit C (the well) and pit E (presented in fig. 22) shows such a trend. Pit C, assumed to be the earliest of the two deposits (although both contained pearlware), tends to surpass pit E in the percentage of earlier type vessels but tends to fall far short in later types, particularly in pearlware. Thus a later date for the deposition of the material in pit E seems all the more probable.

It was also mentioned above that George Jones made Newton Plantation his principal residence until it burned in 1825 and that he probably moved to Wormslow soon afterwards. It is quite possible therefore that after the fire George Jones ceased leasing out Wormslow, tore down the tabby structures near the Narrows, and reused some of the materials in building Wormsloe, the present residence on the plantation site (located one-half mile from the excavation site). In that case, a terminal date of 1820–1825 for the occupation of Wormslow and its subsequent partial destruction seems perfectly sound.

One of the most easily recognized, and unfortunately one of the most predominant, archaeological features found during the course of the excavations was the series of trenches cut across the site, apparently in the 1920s. Three major trenches were found (see fig. 8) : (1) an irregular trench measuring on the average 6' wide and 3' deep cut through the interior of the house; (2) a random trench beginning in bastion II, running along the west wall of the house, narrowing into a 1' wide search trench near the well, and finally ending at what probably had been the second well (discussed above) ; (3) the complete excavation of the fill and floor levels in the tabby cellar located in bastion III. The mixed fill in the trenches in the house and well contained occasional fragmented artifacts, but compared with the quantity of artifacts recovered in undisturbed levels elsewhere on the site, it was obvious that the excavators had made a concerted effort to salvage cultural material. All efforts to locate the artifacts found in the 1920s have failed.

III

Architecture

INTRODUCTION

One of the major objectives of the Wormslow Project was to accumulate enough evidence to make possible an architectural reconstruction of the compound. Historical documents turned out to be of little help on this score; no specific descriptions, drawings, or sketches could be found. Archaeology provided considerable ground level data, but digging also showed that much of the tabby had been removed when the structures were dismantled, and some of the archaeological evidence had been disturbed by earlier modern trenching. However, a portion of the ruins had escaped subsequent disturbances and some sections of the tabby structures were still intact. Therefore, a combination of the archaeological evidence and an architectural study of the standing ruins can provide substantial evidence upon which to base reconstruction.

One can find additional data to aid reconstruction beyond the specific archaeological and architectural evidence found at Wormslow itself. A study of early coastal buildings, in general, and coastal tabby buildings, in particular, can help one visualize eighteenth-century Wormslow—assuming that Noble Jones, the builder, reflected in some measure the architectural trends of his day and area. Therefore the following chapter presents a summary of the archaeologically gathered architectural evidence together with a detailed description of the standing ruins at Wormslow. Then, in light of the physical evidence found at the site, general data pertaining to early house construction and tabby building practices in Georgia have been outlined. An additional detailed analysis of the tabby buildings with which Noble Jones probably had some familiarity has also been included, namely the tabby houses at Frederica, Georgia; the Horton House on Jekyll Island, Georgia; and the tabby houses at St. Augustine, Florida. Finally, a detailed reconstruction has been drawn based on foregoing archaeological and architectural evidence. With the absence of adequate documentary descriptions, however, it cannot be emphasized too strongly that such a reconstruction must remain largely hypothetical in nature, no matter how closely it is tied to the evidence at hand.

In summary, architectural evidence gathered strictly by archaeology indicated that: (1) a rectangular tabby house, constructed circa 1739–1744, with five rooms and an H-shaped hearth had stood at the site, probably until 1820; (2) seemingly an addition was built onto the house, circa 1750–1770; (3) some type of a wattle and daub structure apparently existed at the site prior to the tabby construction.

THE RUINS

Much of the aboveground tabby work had escaped subsequent destruction since the abandonment of the site. Therefore considerable architectural information could be derived from a study of the ruins themselves. Practically all of the outline of the tabby enclosure wall, a considerable section of the east curtain, and portions of two bastions still remain standing today (see figs. 23 and 24). The intact wall sections are 8' high and all of the footings are 1' to 1'2" thick. The fort wall is rectangular in plan, 70' × 80', with a bastion at each corner (see fig. 8). The measurements and the angles of each bastion vary from one to the other, but on an average they have 8'6" to 4' flanks angled from 94° to 102° with the curtains, and

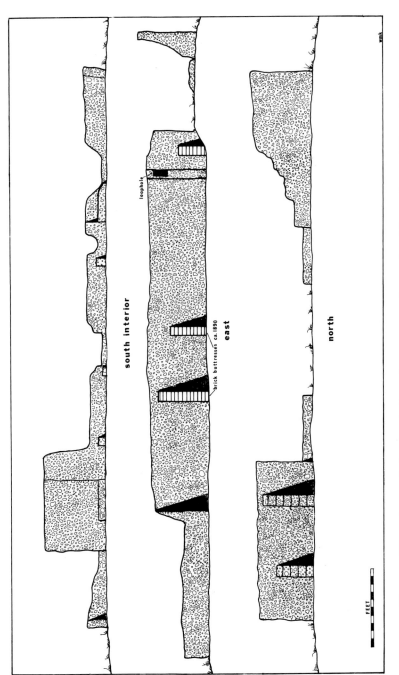

south interior

loophole

brick buttresses ca.1890

east

north

FEET

wmh

Fig. 23. Elevations of the south interior, east, and north tabby ruins at Wormslow.

18'6" × 20' or 21' faces angled at 100°. Allowing for shifts, sags, and erosion in the tabby, the average bastion measures 4' × 18'6" × 20' × 4'. Each of the two south bastions (I and II) has small tabby foundations inside the flanks, averaging 4'6" × 4'6" on the exterior (actually ranging from 4' at a minimum to as much as 5'3" at a maximum, the variation probably having no structural significance). The footings have the same thickness as the rest of the tabby work at the site. Five feet above one of the square footings in the south flank of bastion I, a rectangular window measuring 11' × 1'7" had been built (see fig. 24). A similar opening still remains in the south flank of bastion III.

A square cellar (14' × 14'), also located in bastion III,

Fig. 24. Loophole and tabby footing in bastion I.

still stands (see fig. 25). The north and east walls measure 6′ from top to floor level. A rectangular drop in the wall line at the top of the west wall indicates the location of a 5′6″–wide entrance down into the cellar, and there is similar evidence that another entrance way existed in the northwest corner. The cellar floor had apparently been natural sand. Brick paving measuring 3′ × 7′ was found outside the northwest corner of the structure, immediately in front of the northeast entrance.

A 14′ gap in the tabby fort wall at the center of the north curtain probably indicates the location of the main entrance. This would have been the side of the fort nearest to the approach road from Savannah.

Fig. 25. Tabby cellar in bastion III.

EARLY GEORGIA ARCHITECTURE

The First Dwellings

When seen in light of the early architectural history of Georgia, the details of the Wormslow ruins take on additional meaning. The character of the early architecture of the colony depended upon English building tradition and the nature of the materials at hand. The first houses were probably of a temporary nature and amounted simply to crude huts expediently constructed until more permanent structures could be erected. The structures were probably in part based on traditional English hut construction. However, it is logical to assume that the buildings of the native Indians had a great deal of influence on hut building. The Indian houses of the Georgia coast, built with bent tree framing and wattle and daub painted with oyster-shell whitewash, were no doubt copied for a time by the newly arrived settlers.[1] During the first few years of the settlement of Frederica on St. Simon's Island, Georgia (1736–1740), crude huts of this nature were built, which were described by an early traveler as "thatched bowers . . . a roof raised upon Crutches with Ridgepole and Rafters, railed with small Poles across and Thatching the whole with Palmetto-Leaves." [2] Moreover, wattle and mortar daub wall construction was also used at Frederica in "puncheon construction," where wall posts were set in the ground at about six-inch intervals with wattle and daubing applied to the gaps to form the wall.[3]

The first permanent dwellings in Georgia reflect contemporary English building traditions more directly. In fact the traditional building practices were required by law. The freeholders were ordered to build "one house of brick or framed, square timber work on their respective town Lotts, containing at the least twenty-four feet in length, upon Sixteen in breadth, and eight feet in height" within eighteen months of their arrival.[4] An early sketch of Savannah (1734) shows that these instructions must have been carried out.[5] At least eighty-seven of these houses were standing by that date. The legal Savannah house dimensions, 16′ × 24′, seem to reflect a tendency for Englishmen to build in 8′ bays, a traditional English yeoman's dwelling unit.[6] And the plan (probably consisting of a one-room "hall" on the ground floor with a sleeping loft above), the room sizes, the solid end chimneys, and the roof pitches were all features typical of the small yeoman's dwelling.[7] Therefore the early Savannah house was almost exclusively a traditional English transplant consisting of one story with a central front door flanked by two balanced windows, a gabled roof, and an interior chimney at one end:[8] "a frame of Sawed Timber, 24 × 16 foot, floored with rough Deals [plank sawed to standard dimensions (1¼″ × 9″ × 12′) but not dressed], the sides with feather-edged Boards unplained [rived or sawn from straight-grained log thus producing wedge-shaped clapboards] and the roof shingled."[9]

Domestic Fortification

Because of the colony's defensive purpose, the early settlers of Georgia were concerned with protecting their new homes; therefore, fortification became an early part of the architectural scene. The early Savannah sketch shows that the town was being palisaded, a guardhouse and a "fort" building had been constructed, each individual town lot was enclosed by a wooden fence, and later "some few people had Palisades of turned wood before their Doors."[10] The town of Frederica was fortified accordingly, and many of the out plantations of Georgia were garrisoned or fortified. At Thunderbolt, near Savannah, "five gentlemen . . . have built their houses together, that they might be the more easily fortified which they are with palisades well flanked with pieces of cannon."[11] Moreover a house on Amelia Island, Georgia, was fortified with a battery of cannon in 1741,[12] and

Midway Church (1754) and the "orphan house" at Bethesda (1742) [13] were palisaded or strongly fenced for defensive reasons.

Georgia Georgian

In the latter part of the seventeenth century in the American colonies, the more traditional English building practices began to give way to a new style, the English Georgian. Therefore, as soon as the economic and military situation in Georgia became more stable, the new style became more popular. The Georgian style brought roomier, more formal architecture to Georgia: "the one-room-thick, one-story house in the medieval tradition was superseded by the two-room-thick relatively large two-story residence more typical of the eighteenth century." [14] The change in some cases was almost immediate. A contemporary pointed out that the regulation small planked houses in Savannah were merely the type used for the first forty houses in that city and that "great numbers of much larger [houses] some of them 2 or 3 stories high" had been erected in the three years since the settlement began. [15] Apparently the transition was not so immediate at Frederica. Most of the houses built there were in the traditional rather than in the "new" Georgian style. [16]

As the settlements in Georgia progressed in time and wealth, even the original small structures were expanded horizontally and vertically, becoming "Georgian" at least in plan. Lean-tos and outshuts were added to the original core of the houses, and in some cases dormers and sash windows were added with gambrel and hip roofs replacing the original gables. [17]

Tabby Construction

While the early buildings of Georgia reflect English vernacular and the later English Georgian building styles, the building materials at hand in the infant colony had much to do with the architecture. It is reasonable to assume that most of the early structures were of frame construction, wood probably being the cheapest and easiest to use of the native materials. However, in 1741 Henry Myers, "a very industrious freeholder" of Frederica, wrote: "the people had lately found a better and neater way of building which is by mixing lime and oyster shells, and whilst moist, squeezing them in square boxes of wood which gives them a smooth face and regular shape and was durable." [18] Tabby or "tappy" construction thus became popular in Georgia during the early years of building and could be found on many of the early Georgia structures. The colonists probably learned tabby construction methods from the South Carolinians who had received the first boatload of Georgia settlers at Fort Frederick (Port Royal, South Carolina), which had been constructed of tabby in 1732–1734.[19] The South Carolinians in turn had probably acquired knowledge of tabby construction from the Spanish who had long been using *tapia* (mud or adobe wall construction with lime added) in their buildings. As early as 1509, Ponce de Leon's house at Puerto Rico was made of *tapia,* and the houses of the mission settlement at Santa Elena, later to become the English town of Beaufort, South Carolina, had tabby roofs.[20] By 1764, 140 out of 342 houses in St. Augustine, Florida, were made of tabby, most of which had probably been constructed in the first half of the eighteenth century by the Spanish.[21]

Eighteenth-century tabby construction methods used at St. Augustine are well described in John Bartram's diary:

Most of the common Spanish houses was built of oyster shells and mortar . . . They raised them by setting two boards on edge as wide as they intended the wall, then poured in lime-shell mortar mixed with sand, in which they pounded oyster shells as close as possible. And when that part was set, they raised the planks, and so on till they had raised the wall as high as wanted. This was strong enough to support a terraced chamber floor and a palmetto thatched room and was very tight.[22]

The "boxes," as the "boards on edge" forms were called, were held in place on each course by wooden "needles" (pegs).[23] The "needles" were withdrawn as each pour hardened so that the boxes could be raised to the next level for subsequent pourings. An inspection of the tabby ruins of the Chapel of East at Frogmore, South Carolina (1740), Fort Frederick at Port Royal, South Carolina (1732–1734), the barracks at Frederica (1740), and the Horton brewery at Jekyll Island, Georgia (ca. 1740) showed that the forms used in eighteenth-century tabby construction in coastal Georgia and South Carolina were usually 2' high, thus producing at least 2' courses.[24] The Spanish method used at St. Augustine, however, required smaller forms, and some of the tabby walls incorporated vertical wooden posts for additional strength.[25]

The materials required for tabby construction, equal parts of oyster shell, oyster-shell lime and sand, were well at hand on coastal building sites. The lime was made by calcinating the oyster shells found in abundance on the banks of the numerous saltwater creeks along the South Carolina, Georgia, and Florida coasts. Many prehistoric Indian shell middens were quarried for shells during tabby construction.[26] Sand could be easily obtained by digging 1' 6" below the ground surface anywhere on the coast.

Tabby construction seemed to lose popularity on the coast after about 1760, but the technique was revived again in the first half of the nineteenth century.[27] With the exception of even 1' courses, the nineteenth-century method of tabby construction was similar to the methods of the preceding century. Thomas Spalding, a Sapelo Island planter, described the process in a letter to a friend in 1844 (see fig. 26).[28] Apparently the structure Spalding was describing was begun in 1810 and completed two years later. Although the material

Manner of building.

Two planks as long as convenient to handle, 2 inches thick and about 12 inches wide, are made to unite and to go the round of your building. These planks are kept apart by spreader pins with

a double head as thus , the first head keeps the outer plank in its place, the last with the pin run through the point, keeps the inner plank firm while the workmen are filling in the material and setting it down, either with a spade or a light rammer, which, if shells, bring these into a flat position. Then, the planks at the ends are let into each other

thus: ⟨drawing⟩ with an iron wire ⟨drawing⟩

with eye to draw it out at each round of Tabby. The corners

of the building are thus: ⟨drawing⟩ the same kind of

iron wire binding the sides together.

All that is necessary when you construct doors or windows, is to drop a short board across the wall between the outer and inner planks and steady it with two poles, to be drawn out at each round and replaced at the next, and so continue until you have reached the height you intend your doors and windows. When you then drop your Lintall into the Tabby Box so as to secure the next round of Tabby your wall then becomes an intire whole.

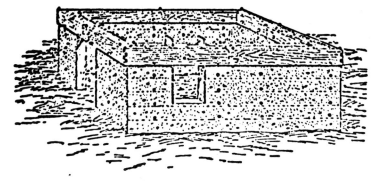

Fig. 26. Description of tabby construction by Thomas Spalding, 1844 (Coulter, *Georgia's Disputed Ruins*, p. 74: by permission of the University of North Carolina Press).

was durable, tabby was extremely slow in setting; therefore, tabby buildings would require a long construction period. At any rate the advantage of durability apparently offset the problem of slow construction as the number of eighteenth- and nineteenth-century tabby ruins of the Georgia coast indicates.[29]

EARLY COLONIAL TABBY ARCHITECTURE

A study and synthesis of the features of eighteenth-century tabby-house remains at Frederica and Jekyll Island, Georgia, and a review of colonial houses at St. Augustine, Florida, can provide a reasonable picture of what a typical eighteenth-century tabby house may have looked like (see figs. 27, 28, 29, and 30). Synthetic analysis of early colonial tabby structures in turn provides additional evidence on which to base a documentary reconstruction of Wormslow.

The tabby houses of St. Augustine were built almost exclusively in the period 1703–1763. Most of the houses followed the one- or two-celled simple plan discussed above. However, a considerable number of houses at St. Augustine were built on a more sophisticated plan (called by architects the St. Augustine plan) which basically consisted of "a simple rectangle of from two to four rather spacious rooms, with a loggia or porch . . . facing south or east so that in the summer the prevailing southeast airs ventilated the large rooms and . . . porches"[30] (see fig. 28). The houses built on the St. Augustine plan ranged in size from 24′ × 36′ to 42′ × 45′ with the main rooms measuring from 16′ × 16′ to 22 × 25′.[31]

No houses remain standing at Frederica, but archaeological excavations conducted there in the 1950s uncovered twelve house ruins complete enough to exhibit plan characteristics. Of the twelve, half were vernacular in style, two

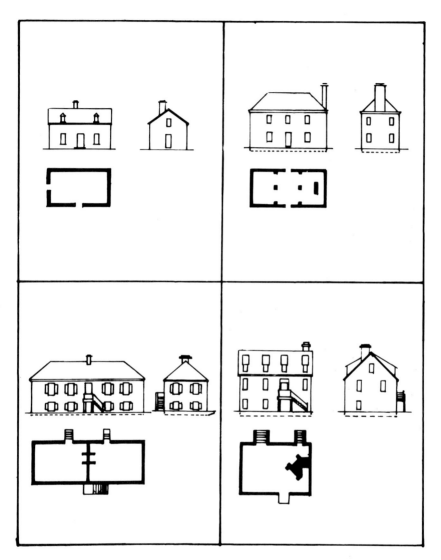

Fig. 27. Floor plans and conjectural reconstruction of the tabby houses at Frederica, Ga., ca. 1740 (after Manucy).

had additions that showed them to be transitional, and four were clearly Georgian. All of the ruins in the Georgian style were made of tabby, while only two of the other styles were made of that material (see fig. 27). The overall dimensions ranged in size from 32' × 26' to 48' × 22'. Not enough evidence remained of the partitions to estimate the room sizes.[32]

On Jekyll Island the ruins of the two-story tabby residence of Captain William Horton, probably built soon after 1742, remain reasonably intact and provide some insight into the appearance of eighteenth-century tabby houses of the Georgia coast (see fig. 30). It is basically a vernacular plan, with a hall and parlor on the ground floor. Its overall dimensions, however, 41'6" × 18', would probably classify it as the larger transitional style. The main "hall" measures 25' × 15'.[33]

Stories

Tabby buildings at St. Augustine ranged from one story to two and a half stories, but the majority of the houses built on the St. Augustine plan were one and a half stories or more.[34] The one-and-a-half-story house was definitely popular during British times (after 1763), and there is indirect evidence that this type existed earlier, during the Spanish period.[35] The tabby part of the facade could vary in one-and-a-half- and two-story structures, some having tabby walls only on the first floor level with others having one and a half or two full stories of tabby construction. The width of the tabby wall determined the height of the house. A 9" to 11" tabby wall with incorporated wooden posts was standard for a one-story house while a two-story tabby wall would be at least 15" thick.[36]

According to archaeological and historical evidence, one-and-a-half-, two-, and three-story tabby houses were built at Frederica. The tabby buildings in the "new" Georgian style were all more than one story; one being one and a half stories, two being two stories, and one three stories. The three-story building had a wall thickness of 18" while the walls of the

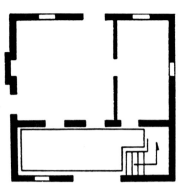

Fig. 28. One-and-a-half-story colonial house at 46 Bridge Street, St. Augustine, Fla. (Manucy, *Houses of St. Augustine,* page 57: by permission of the St. Augustine Historical Society).

Fig. 29. St. Augustine–plan house at 42 Spanish Street, St. Augustine, Fla. (Manucy, *Houses of St. Augustine,* page 75: by permission of the St. Augustine Historical Society).

others were 14″ thick.[37] One-story houses had walls no more than 12″ thick. How many stories of these houses were actually of tabby and how much of the upper levels of the multistoried houses were frame is not known, but it seems likely that tabby was used only for the first floor levels in the two-story houses.

The wall thicknesses of the two-story Horton House give more credibility to this view. The wall thickness on the lower story is 18″ while the upper story wall is only 1′ thick.[38] From this and the evidence at Frederica and St. Augustine, it is reasonable to conclude that tabby structures with a wall less than 18″ but more than 1′ thick probably would be more than one story high and have only one story of tabby with frame construction above.

Wall Finish

The walls of the tabby houses of St. Augustine, Frederica, and the Horton House were all finished both inside and outside with a thin coating of plaster which was subsequently whitewashed.[39] The smooth plaster surfaces served as a water-proofing device and helped to keep the houses clean. Moreover, walls of tabby without a plaster coating can prove dangerous since the razor-sharp edges of the shell aggregate can cut cloth and flesh upon even the slightest contact.

Floors

A variety of flooring material was used in eighteenth-century tabby houses, but tabby floors were the most common. At St. Augustine it was unusual for archaeologists to uncover only one tabby floor in the excavations. Usually several layers of tabby floors, one built directly on the next, were found, indicating that when the old floor became rough and pitted, the usual practice was to lay an entirely new one down instead of repairing the first. One excavated structure had at least four tabby floor levels, all built in the period circa 1650–1780. The floors were usually 2″ to 3″ thick and were constructed upon a 1″ or 2″ base of packed shell chips. The wet floors were then tamped so that the aggregate material (shells) would sink to the bottom, thus producing a smooth surface.[40] Five of the six tabby houses found at Frederica also had tabby floors, while the one exception had a wooden floor, and one house had one tile-floored room.[41] The Horton House had a tabby floor during its earlier occupation. It was 3″ thick and built upon 1″ to 7″ of tamped clay.[42]

Doorways

There is a considerable variation in the makeup and size of doorways in eighteenth-century tabby houses. The doorways of the houses of St. Augustine ranged from 3′ to 4′ in width and the door frame often consisted of two long doorposts (jambs) set firmly into the masonry during the construction of the walls. The post-jambs were usually connected at the top by a simple wooden lintel. When the English occupied St. Augustine, the post-jamb construction was abandoned for the standard British rectangular box frame which was much easier to replace.[43] At Frederica the wooden door frames were built directly against the masonry jambs and apparently no post-jambs were used. Front doors at Frederica ranged from 3' to 7'2" in width. The widest doorways probably had transoms and sidelights. Back doors measured from a minimum of 3' to a maximum of 5'6" wide. Inconsistency in the width of doorways seemed to be the rule there.[44] The front door of the Horton House measures 4'3" and the back 2'11". Here the sills were faced with brick.[45]

Chimneys

Chimneys on eighteenth-century tabby houses varied considerably in size and shape. Not many chimneys were built in St. Augustine by the Spanish before 1763. After that date the English built their brick or shell stone chimneys onto the new structures or added them to already existing houses constructed by the Spanish. The chimneys were not always placed on the gable wall as was generally the custom in English construction; thus, outside, inside, and flush stacks occur as often as the conventional gable end stacks. The chimneys at St. Augustine were not massive, and at least thirteen different crown moldings were used by the builders.[46] Four brick or brick and tabby chimney foundations were found in the course of the excavations at Frederica. There is considerable variation in hearth sizes and exterior dimensions. They range in size from a 2' × 4' hearth having an exterior dimension of 2'8" × 6'3" to an H-shaped chimney with a 2'8" × 4'6" hearth with exterior dimensions of 7' × 7'8". One house had a tabby chimney with a brick hearth while the rest of the chimneys and hearths were made entirely of brick. The relatively small chimney bases indicate that the stacks were not massive.[47] The chimneys of the Horton House were built flush with the outside walls at each end of the structure, having hearths of 4'10" × 1'7" at one end and 4'10" × 2' at the other, with overall exterior dimensions of 7'2" × 3'2" and 7'2" × 3'9" respectively.[48]

Height

Eleven feet was the standard wall height for substantial one-story masonry buildings, 14'2" for one-and-a-half-story houses and 19'7" for two-story structures at St. Augustine. One two-story frame dwelling built there in 1779 had an overall size of 20' × 32' and had 19'-high walls.[49] Conjectural reconstructions made of the Frederica ruins show walls 10' high for one-story houses, 14' for two-story houses and 18' to 20' for three-story houses.[50] The walls of the two-story Horton House now stand 18', probably their original height.[51] The total height of tabby buildings of course depended on the type and pitch of the roof. However, the gable roof houses of St. Augustine average 16' for a one-story house, 20' for a one-and-a-half-story house, about 25' for a two-story house, and 32' for a three-story house.[52] The heights of the reconstructions of the Frederica houses are about the same, and thus these houses were probably based on existing models in St. Augustine.

Windows

Windows were usually symmetrically placed on colonial tabby buildings. At St. Augustine the common arrangement on one-story houses was to flank central front doors with two windows of equal size and spacing. On houses of one and a half and two stories, the same first-floor arrangement was retained and balanced by placing three smaller windows on the upper story, directly over the openings of the ground floor. There is no standard window size at St. Augustine. The windows there range from 27" to 44" in width, but second story windows are usually proportionately smaller than those on the first floor and street floor. Street and yard windows are usually large and high on the east and south sides of the house.[53] One ruin at Frederica retained structural window evidence. Several windowsill impressions in the tabby basement footings indicated that it had had windows 30" wide framed with jambs 3' above the tabby floor. If the ceiling height had been the standard 8', the windows could not have been more than 5' high. The windows of the reconstruction drawings of the Frederica houses are symmetrically placed much as those of St. Augustine houses, with second-story openings usually proportionately smaller than those on the first floor.[54] Glazed double-hung window sashes were common at St. Augustine, at least after 1763, replacing the Spanish inside shutters. They commonly had six or nine glass panels arranged nine over six on the first floor and six over six on the second.[55]

Much window glass was recovered in the course of the excavations at Frederica, suggesting that the windows there too were in the typical double-hung sash mode of the English Georgian style. Judging from the great number of shutter latches found, it is quite probable that most of the windows at Frederica were either "glazed, barred, or open" with outside shutters.[56] Apparently the windows of the Horton House were glazed and shuttered in a like manner.

Roofs

The tabby houses of St. Augustine had flat, gabled, or hipped roofs covered with either thatch or wooden shingles, and occasionally tabby was used on flat roofs. Before circa 1760, most of the roofs were flat or sloped at either 53° or 45°. The steepest slope was more of a vernacular construction, and it provided more headroom in the sleeping loft. However, in the period circa 1760–1800, the common roof slopes became 45°, 40°, and even 30° and hipped roofs became popular.[57] Very little information concerning the appearance of the roofs at Frederica is available, but based on eighteenth-century practice and floor plans, it is likely that the tabby

houses there had both gabled and hipped roofs with from
30° to 45° pitches. Historical records show that most of the
roofs at Frederica were covered with wooden shingles.[58] The
records leave little doubt that the Horton House had a
hipped roof, at least by 1787, and probably earlier.[59] Cornices
were rarely used on the houses of St. Augustine, while typical
English box cornices are conjectured for the houses of Frederica and the Horton House.

Dormers

Dormers seem to be a late colonial feature of the houses at
St. Augustine. Both shed and gabled dormer roofs are commonly found there, the former type, usually quite small, is
generally found on one-and-a-half-story houses, while the
latter type is usually larger and found on two-story houses.
One shed roofed dormer type was often built partially
through the roof plate on frame or tabby and frame structures.[60] Reconstruction drawings of the Frederica houses show
both gable and shed roofed dormers, and evidence suggests
that the shed roof type was probably the earliest form used
there.[61] The Horton House probably did not have dormers.[62]

RECONSTRUCTION OF WORMSLOW

Wattle and Daub Huts

The wattle and daub mortar found on the site in association
with pretabby occupation suggests that the builder first constructed a crude workman's hut, similar to the earliest huts
of Savannah and Frederica, at the site before the tabby construction began. It stands to reason that such a structure or
structures would be built to house the workers who had to
live at the site during the long tabby construction period. Although no structural outlines of such huts were found inside
the tabby ruins, it is reasonable to assume that they were

located outside the building area. During the construction of nearby Bethesda in 1740–1742, the workmen's huts are shown on a map done by Noble Jones as being outside the fenced or palisaded complex.[63] There is no reason to believe that Jones himself did not use a similar arrangement for his construction, which was taking place at the same time. Moreover, the one eighteenth-century description of Wormslow relates that the soldiers garrisoned at the guardhouse lived in "huts" near the Wormslow house, and perhaps they took over the original workmen's structures for their own use.[64] In fact the soldiers themselves may well have been the workers (see chapter 1, Noble Jones's Ownership).

The Tabby House

More definite data is available for the reconstruction of the house at Wormslow (see figs. 31 and 32). The overall dimensions of the building ruins, 32′ × 24′, show that it was exactly double the size of the floor space of the earliest required houses of Savannah. In plan therefore the house must have been more in the newer and roomier Georgian style, which was common to the tabby houses of contemporary Frederica. However, the 8′ increments and the main "hall" room with its fireplace and the adjacent smaller "parlor" show that the vernacular tradition was not eliminated entirely. But the addition of the two small storage rooms (rooms 3 and 4) and the narrow room in the northeast corner of the building (room 5) illustrate the tendency toward the Georgian style; and in fact the entire plan is strikingly similar to one example of the advanced St. Augustine–plan houses of Florida.[65] However, viewed in light of the St. Augustine–plan houses, Wormslow was comparatively small, although the size of the main "hall," 22′ × 15′, is similar to some St. Augustine structures. Moreover, the "room" is almost the same size as the "hall" at the larger two-story Horton House.

Based on the ratio of wall width to stories found on other

Fig. 30. A conjectural reconstruction of Horton House on Jekyll Island, Ga., ca. 1742 (Everette Fauber, Jr., "A Comprehensive Report and a Proposal for the Restoration of Captain Horton's House on Jekyll Island, Georgia, 1967," p. 124: by permission of the Jekyll Island State Park Authority).

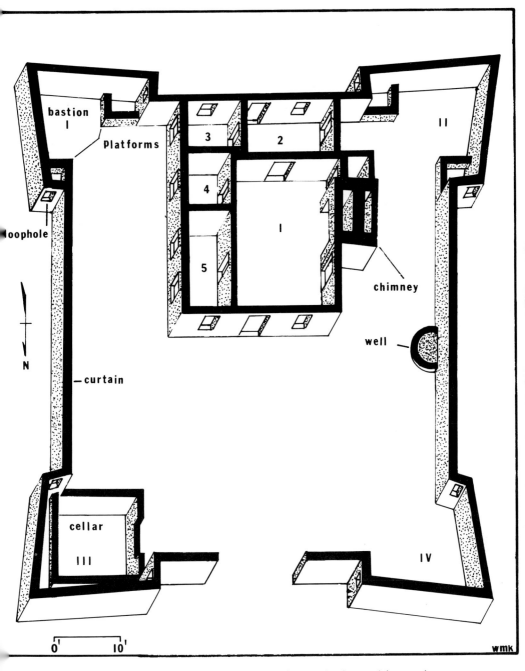

Fig. 31. A conjectural reconstruction of the tabby ruins at Wormslow.

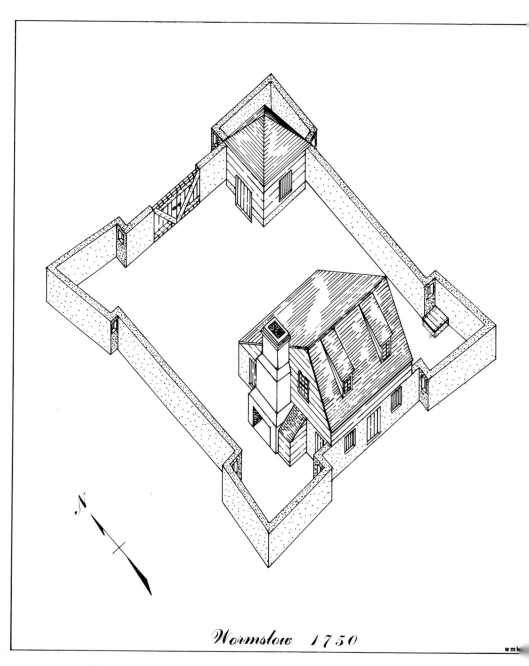

Wormslow 1750

Fig. 32. A conjectural reconstruction of Wormslow, ca. 1750.

colonial tabby houses, it is reasonable to conclude that the 1′ to 1′2″ thick footings found at Wormslow supported at least a one-and-a-half-story house. It is also reasonable to assume that the tabby portion of the house was only 8′ high, the same height as the fort wall which also served as the south wall of the house. This height would be considerably lower than the tabby walls at St. Augustine, but the remaining height was probably built of frame construction, bringing it up to the standard 14′ required for one-and-a-half-story houses. The unweathered portions of the footings showed that the tabby walls had been smoothed with plaster and whitewashed in the same manner as the other tabby houses of the period.

Tabby, apparently brick tile, and wood were used as floor coverings at Wormslow. The tabby floors in rooms 2, 4, and 5 were the same thickness (about 3″) as the contemporary tabby floors at St. Augustine and at the Horton House, and they had probably been finished by working the shell aggregate to the bottom, much as the Spanish did at St. Augustine. But there the similarity to other tabby floors ends. Unlike St. Augustine and the Horton House, the Wormslow floors were laid on a 1′-thick layer of clean yellow sand and were apparently laid in separate rectangular wooden forms, with the form boards left in place to serve as part of the floor. The floor of the main room (room 1) was apparently made up of square brick tiles 3/4″ × 1′4″ × ? laid on clean yellow sand and a thin spread of marl mortar. One house at Frederica had a room floored with brick tiles, but floors of this type in a tabby house were uncommon. Impressions in the tabby footings of room 3 suggest that it had had a wooden floor; thus it was probably a dry storage room, possibly for flour.[66] The size of the room, 8′ × 6′6″, would have rendered it too small for a living space. Room 4 was smaller yet, and therefore it too must have been used only for storage. Its tabby floor would have been adequate for cooler storage.

The remains of the partition foundations show that they had supported frame construction. Impressions in the tabby indicated that 4"-wide wooden sills had been used and that the corner posts were of 4" × 4" stock placed in the ground through the unset tabby. Fragments of plaster suggest that the partition walls were lathed with 1"-wide wooden strips which had been covered with ⅜" of fine plaster. The plaster showed that it had also been whitewashed. In rooms 4 and 5 enough of the tabby floor remained to show that it had been laid on top of the edge of the tabby partition footing, flush with the wooden partition sills. The ceilings were probably lathed and plastered in the same manner as the partitions, although no direct evidence was found to support the supposition.

Impressions of four doorways were found in the house footings. The square holes on each side of the south and southwest doorways and the square hole on the south side of the doorway located just north of the chimney indicate that the door frames were constructed in the post-jamb Spanish manner. Since the jambs were of 4" × 4" stock (the size of the holes in the tabby), the front door (the door on the south wall facing the water approach to the site) would have been 3′4″ wide, while the other double post-jamb doorway (on the west wall) would have been smaller, measuring 2′8″ across. The single post-jamb doorway must have had the largest opening, measuring 3′8″ wide. The other doorway on the west wall, just south of the chimney, had originally been the same size as the entrance on the north side of the hearth (3′8″), but it had subsequently been narrowed by the addition of a course of brick along the south jamb. Consequently this doorway was the narrowest of all (assuming the frame was of 3″ stock), measuring only 2′3″ wide. The house probably had an additional doorway on the north wall, directly opposite the main south door. A posthole in line with the wall footing suggests that the north door was also of post-jamb construction and probably matched the south door in width. It is probable that all of the doors were 7' high, the standard at St. Augustine.

The placement of the chimney on the long axis of the house (i.e., on the west wall), its H-shape with opposite fireplaces, and its relatively massive proportions (10' × 6'6") are not as typical of other tabby buildings as the Wormslow house plan and its other construction details. Usually chimney foundations were smaller; usually H-shaped chimneys were located at the center of a house so that its opposite fireplaces would be in separate rooms; and usually a single outside chimney would be located on one of the narrow walls of a rectangular building, running up to the gable end of the roof. However, since the logical direction for the front of the Wormslow house would have been toward the water passage to the south, it is reasonable to assume that the gable ends of the roof would have been on the east and west walls. And if the chimney had been built either to provide an outside working hearth or with an addition to the house in mind (thus eventually incorporating the additional hearth *inside* the addition), then these unusual features of the chimney location and plan do not pose too great a problem in reconstruction. There are many possible styles of chimney "weathering" that could have been employed at Wormslow. There is a precedent for practically every conceivable method. (See figs. 33 and 34). The cap could have had one of several moldings, all typical of the period.[67] It may have had simply a one-course band near the top, one of the easiest molding styles to construct.

The small, roughly made, square brick foundation built next to the chimney base was probably the footing for a wooden closet or woodshed, entered through the narrowest doorway on the west wall. Such a feature was commonly built next to chimneys and usually had a shed roof. (See fig. 34.) It was added to the house sometime after the tabby construction

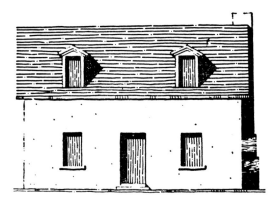

Fig. 33. Colonial house, showing two-stage chimney weatherings, 250 St. George Street, St. Augustine, Fla. (Manucy, *Houses of St. Augustine,* page 57: by permission of the St. Augustine Historical Society).

Fig. 34. Chimney weathering detail and attached shed on Hanover House, Clemson, S.C., 1716 (Forman, *Architecture of the Old South,* p. 179: by permission of Harvard University Press).

period, probably at the same time that the doorway was narrowed with brick. The narrowness of the door seems to rule out the possibility that this feature may have been an exterior footing for a stairway to the second floor. Evidence of an interior stairway was not found, but it was probably located in the northwest corner of the main room.

If the house at Wormslow was a one-and-a-half-story building, then it typically would have been 20′ high. And if the gable ends of the roof were located on the longest walls of the house, as indicated by the position of the front door and the chimney, then it is quite possible that the house had an off-center, saltboxlike (catslide) roof. If that were the case, the house would have had a long catslide at the back pitched at 30° and a shorter 45° pitched roof in front with dormer windows. The catslide roof with dormers at the front was not uncommon for houses of Georgia or the southeast. A mid-eighteenth-century frame plantation home in the Savannah area Wild Heron (ca. 1756) incorporates a variation of the saltbox with front dormers (see fig. 35). A frame house still standing in Savannah at 556 Selma Street (probably of eighteenth-century date) is built in exactly the same manner (see fig. 36). Another similar house, made of tabby, Button Gwinnett's house on St. Catherine's Island, Georgia, has the same type of roof.

The Wormslow roof was probably covered with wooden shingles and typically would not have had a cornice. The dormers were probably of the earliest shed-roofed type so common on early Georgia and St. Augustine one-and-a-half-story buildings. The pitch of the shed would have been 30° (any less tended to leak).

No archaeological evidence was found indicating the position and size of the windows of the house, but contemporary architectural data suggests that they would have been symmetrically placed with two windows flanking the main north and south doorways. The room arrangement of the house suggests that there may have been four evenly spaced windows along the east wall. The windows on the south front were probably made quite small for purposes of defense, while those along the east wall would have been larger for ventilation. In addition to the windows in the dormers on the second floor, there may have been small windows on each gable end of the house to allow for cross ventilation. The large quantity of window glass recovered in the excavations indicates that the windows were glazed and that they were more than likely the typical double hung English sash types with six over nine glass panels in each opening on the ground floor and six over six on the second floor. For defensive purposes, however, the two windows on the south wall were probably originally barred and shuttered.

The later frame addition probably made to the west wall

Fig. 35. Wild Heron Plantation House, near Savannah, Ga., 1756.

Fig. 36. Early house in Savannah at 556 Selma Street, showing typical Georgia coastal roof and dormer construction.

of the house must have been a simple one-room outshut. It is quite likely that the kitchen activities were moved to this room, making use of the west hearth and oven of the main chimney. The addition would have been quite simple to build on to the house, merely requiring a north and south frame wall running out to join the tabby fort wall, a wooden floor, and a lean-to roof connecting the west gable end of the house to the top of the tabby wall. It also may have had a small wooden stoop at the main north entrance, as indicated by two postholes found during the course of the excavations.

Because of the almost unbearable summer climate of the Georgia coast, it was quite common for houses to have an open porch on one or more sides. There is indirect evidence that Wormslow had a porch or a "piazza" by 1763, if John Bartram had in fact stopped to see Noble Jones that year during his travels.[68] If Wormslow did have a porch, then it is reasonable to assume that it would have been located at the front of the house facing Skidaway Narrows. However, no evidence in the masonry indicated such a porch and the excavations were not extended outside the tabby ruins in that area. If the building did have a porch and if it was located on the south front, then it was probably added much later than the tabby construction period. The structure would have been outside the tabby defenses of the site, so it was probably not until fortification was no longer considered important that the porch was built.

The Tabby Fortifications

The least hypothetical feature of any Wormslow reconstruction is the fort enclosure itself. About one-quarter of the wall remains standing, and almost all of the remaining wall footings are in excellent condition. Based on the ruins still standing, one can quite reasonably assume that the fort wall was 8′ in height all around and that it had a 14′-wide main entrance gate on the north curtain. Moreover each bastion flank wall probably had a loophole in it, as indicated by the two examples still standing at the site. Bastions I and II probably had tabby-based wooden firing platforms in front of each loophole, and bastion III probably had an elevated wooden floor in front of the south loophole. No evidence of similar platform foundations was found in bastion IV, but there is little reason to believe that loopholes were not located there; the whole purpose of the bastion would have been defeated without them.

There is very little specific information describing eighteenth-century fortified houses of the period, but it was undoubtedly unique to find an early plantation with such a sophisticated defense system as that constructed at Wormslow. The fort at Frederica, made of earth and palisades, was

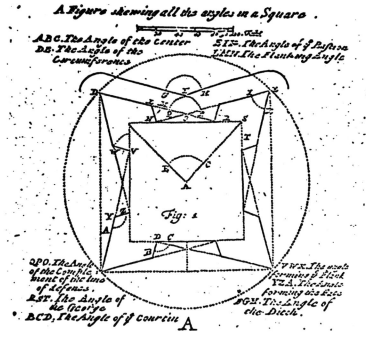

Fig. 37. Vauban's plan for constructing a square bastioned fort, 1693 (Vauban, *A Method of Fortification*).

similar in shape, being a typical "square" rampart in the Vauban manner.[69] But the walls at Wormslow were merely 14" of tabby which could not possibly have withstood the weakest cannonading. Its rectangular shape is also odd and rendered the structure geometrically difficult to build. It was apparently easy to lay off the bastion angles of a square fort, but a rectangular fort would have been more difficult (see fig. 37). This may explain the resulting irregularities in the bastion sizes and angles. Apparently the builders did not have access to Oglethorpe's copy of the Vauban manual for building such fortifications. If so, many of the errors would have been avoided. Therefore the fort probably was merely one man's uneducated conception of what an eighteenth-century square bastioned fort should look like.

The Outbuilding

Evidence of one other structure, the tabby cellar in bastion III, can provide for conjectural reconstruction. The square cellar probably had a frame or tabby one-story outbuilding over it. The upper room could have been used for dry food or tool storage and the cellar for a cold storage bin. It probably had a typical "hipped" roof commonly found on square outbuildings in eighteenth-century Georgia and the southeast (see fig. 38). It would have been roofed with wooden shingles, and in addition to the wide bulkhead entrance on the west wall, it would have had a door (most likely on the south wall) to the ground-level floor. It probably would have had another doorway from the building into the bastion (located in the northwest corner, in front of the brick paved step into the bastion). It is likely that the structure did not have windows.[70]

Method of Construction

An examination of the tabbywork itself—as seen in the light of eighteenth-century descriptions of tabby construction

Fig. 38. Tabby smokehouse, St. Catherine's Island, Ga.

methods—makes it possible to indicate the essentials of the building process. Impressions in the east curtain wall show that the builders used relatively wide wooden forms made of boards measuring 6″ × 12′. The resulting tabby courses averaged about 2′ high, shown above to be typical of eighteenth-century tabby construction. The forms had apparently been held in place by crudely rounded wooden pegs about 1″ in diameter, spaced at regular intervals of 3′8″. Most of the holes made in the wall by the removal of each peg were later backfilled with mortar, then capped with a fragment of brick. The 2′ coursing, the 3′8″ spacing of the pegs, and mortar and brick backfilling were all common building practices used in eighteenth-century tabby work. Fort Frederick at Port Royal, South Carolina, the tabby barracks at Frederica, and the ruins of the brewery near the Horton House, all clearly show that the tabby had been laid in 2′ courses. The peg spacings of the barracks and the brewery were all between 3′ and 4′.

Brickbat and mortar backfilling were used on the Horton House.

The oyster shells to make the lime and to serve as the aggregate for the Wormslow tabby had apparently been quarried about fifty yards southeast of the building site on the banks of the Skidaway Narrows. At least three 30' × 30' pits are still visible on the banks. The shells were probably accumulated by prehistoric Indians, if the Guale Indian pot sherd sealed into the east curtain wall is any indicator.

According to the nineteenth-century tabby builder Thomas Spalding, 10 bushels each of lime, sand, shell, and water made 16 cubic feet of tabby; it took six hands three days to complete a course (making two rounds a week), and the workers averaged laying 30 cubic feet of tabby a day, mixing one day and pouring two days. The work season was halted during the fall because of the tropical storms.[71] There probably was at least 3200 cubic feet of tabby used at Wormslow, which, according to Spalding's description, would represent a total of 8000 bushels of lime, sand, shell, and water. Obviously Noble Jones must have had a considerable labor force for the undertaking. Since slaves were not allowed in the colony until 1750 (probably long after Wormslow was constructed), and since Noble Jones had very few reliable servants before he acquired his slaves, it is conceivable that he used some of the ten "marines" who had been placed under his command to guard the Narrows for the tabby work.[72] Assuming that only about half of the men would be available for his "private enterprise" at any one time, and assuming that it in fact took at least six hands to construct with tabby (as Spalding suggests), and assuming that the climate would only allow a maximum of a five-day work week (tabby could not be worked in the rain), then it probably would have taken at least five uninterrupted months to complete the tabby work. However, in actuality, it probably took considerably longer to build Wormslow. The records show that the marines and Noble Jones himself were frequently employed in a scoutboat delivering mail and transporting people either to South Carolina or Frederica, thus leaving relatively little time for building.[73]

Conclusion

Certainly reconstructed Wormslow with its yeoman-like house incorporated into a rectangular bastioned wall appears

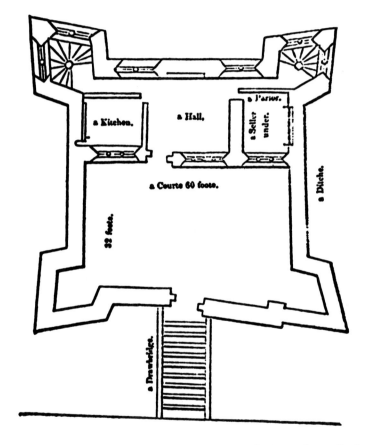

Fig. 39. An English ironmonger's "bawn" in Northern Ireland, ca. 1615 (Garvan, *Architecture and Town Planning in Colonial Connecticut,* p. 127: by permission of Yale University Press).

to be a far cry from the modern conception of a typical eighteenth-century southern plantation. But it was probably not as unusual as it first appears. Research shows that many early Georgia settlements and plantations were fortified; the buffer role of the colony made such defenses practically mandatory. Security in the mode of traditional western-European fortification must have appealed to Englishmen settling the Georgia no-man's-land. In that sense the foreign environment of Georgia molded one transplanted English settler's plantation development scheme.

Further research suggests that the reaction of Jones and other colonists to the hostile physical and political surroundings was not all that unique nor confined to the eighteenth century or the American colonies. Over a century earlier the English settlers of Ulster in Northern Ireland responded to their insecurity by constructing "bawns" or fortified residences (see fig. 39).[74] It could not be mere chance that the plan uncovered at Wormslow could almost directly overlay an Irish fortified residence of the early seventeenth century (compare fig. 8 with figs. 32 and 39).

At any rate it is indeed fortunate that Noble Jones chose to build his "bawn" with durable tabby, thus enabling at least one fortified Georgia plantation plan to survive.

IV

The Artifacts

The artifacts recovered during the course of the excavations at Wormslow comprise an interesting and varied collection of eighteenth- and early nineteenth-century cultural material. The bulk of the collection dates from the last half of the occupation period, circa 1770–1820. However, enough was found in earlier deposits to provide a reasonable picture of what types of artifacts were used at the site from the earliest settlement. Most of the artifacts were ceramic or wine bottle fragments, but many metal objects were recovered along with some building materials and animal bones.

Ceramics

Representative sherds of most of the major English ceramic types manufactured in the eighteenth and early nineteenth centuries were found, including samples of coarse earthenware, slipware, delftware, white saltglazed stoneware, creamware, and pearlware (see figs. 46–49). Moreover, one sherd of English porcelain was recovered, and pieces of Chinese export porcelain, German gray saltglazed stoneware, and occasional sherds of prehistoric and Indian pottery in European forms were also found (see figs. 47, 49, and 52). Most of the ceramic remains from the earliest deposits (ca. 1737–1744, i.e., from pit A, the subfloor of the house, and various construction debris deposits) consisted of coarse earthenware mixed with some delftware, a few sherds of early white saltglazed stoneware, and yellow slipware. Generally speaking, delftware was comparatively scarce, while coarse earthenware and slipware were predominant in most of the deposits regardless of date.

Fig. 40. A representative collection of artifacts found at Wormslow including: wine bottles of the period 1730–1745 and 1755–
1775, creamware cup and saucer, 1765–1785 (lower left), eighteenth-century bone-handled fork, pewter spoon, clay tobacco
pipe, brass candlestick, and a white saltglazed stoneware cup and
scratch blue saucer, 1750–1775 (right).

During the last half of the occupation period, (represented
by the material in pits C and E) much white saltglazed stoneware, both molded and scratch blue, was used at the site, as
well as fine creamware and some Chinese porcelain.

The bulk of the Wormslow ceramic collection is made up
of numerous varieties of coarse earthenware (see fig. 46).

Most of the sherds are from milk pans, but other vessel forms include mugs, pitchers, storage jars, small pots, and crude unglazed bottles. The coarse earthenware body colors range from red to beige, and the glazes are rust to greenish yellow in color. Most sherds are lead glazed on one side only. Although it is impossible to be certain, there is a good possibility that some of the coarse earthenware was locally made. One mottled green and red lead-glazed mug (see fig. 46, no. 22) is strikingly similar to vessels made by the Moravians in Salem, North Carolina, in the second half of the eighteenth century.

Several varieties of slipware were found throughout the site (see fig. 47, nos. 15–19). In the fill in the well (pit C) at least twenty-six fragmented slipware vessels were recovered, most of which have a yellow body decorated with a dark-brown trailed slip. Slipware vessel forms include posset pots, bowls, and notched-rim dishes.

Fragments of delftware vessels were recovered, but they were comparatively scarce (see fig. 47, no. 9–14 and fig. 49, nos. 8–12). A few sherds of large bowls were found along with a hand-painted cup base, a pinkish white drug jar, two light blue ointment-pots, and a few plate fragments.

Varieties of white saltglazed stoneware were found in most of the deposits on the site, particularly in the well fill, where at least twenty-two white saltglazed vessels were recovered (see fig. 48, nos. 1–11). Most of the sherds were from plain white cups and saucers. However, a few examples of drab white saucers decorated with scratch blue floral designs were also found. Saltglazed plates with rims molded in the dot, diaper, and basket pattern, and the bead and reel pattern were also found along with a plain white teapot lid.

Other types of stoneware found at Wormslow include Westerwald gray saltglazed stoneware, English brown salt-glazed stoneware (see fig. 47, nos. 1–4), and red stoneware (see fig. 49, no. 7). Of particular significance were fragments of a Westerwald gray stoneware chamberpot and storage jar, both decorated with bands of cobalt blue, a neck and handle sherd from a brown stoneware bottle, and the mouth and shoulder from a brown stoneware storage jar. Fragments from a dry-body red stoneware teapot decorated with sprig-molded foliate designs and horses were found in a mid-eighteenth-century deposit.

Numerous sherds of English Queensware or cream-colored ware were recovered (see fig. 48, nos. 12–25). Fragments from cups and saucers, bowls, basins, plates, teapots, and pitchers were found, some featuring relief molded pearl or bead and reel borders and others featuring hand-painted floral designs or underglaze marbling. A creamware pitcher decorated with a black transfer-printed design showing two sailors in front of what appears to be a tavern with the caption "The wand'ring Sai[lor]" was recovered in an early nineteenth-century deposit. The creamware plate fragments found at the site were either molded in the traditional Royal pattern or were plain. Some sherds of early creamware covered with an emerald green glaze, usually attributed to Josiah Wedgwood's early pottery, were also found. One such plate rim had been molded in the barley pattern. A single sherd of Wheildon-Wedgwood cauliflower molded creamware, probably of the late 1750s or early 1760s, was also recovered.

The Wormslow collection also contains some pearlware, most of which had come from plain or hand-painted cups, saucers, and bowls. A few sherds were found with chinoiserie transfer-printed scenes featuring traditional willow pattern borders (see fig. 48, no. 26). Three rim sherds from a shell-edged plate banded in blue were also found.

Sherds of Chinese porcelain cups, saucers, and bowls were found at Wormslow, most of which had been decorated in hand-painted cobalt-blue floral or pastoral designs (see fig. 49, nos. 1–4 and 6). A few minute fragments of more elaborate Chinese porcelain with overglaze red designs were also

recovered along with part of the base from an English porcelain cup decorated in deep underglaze blue (see fig. 49, no.
5). Comparatively speaking, however, very few sherds of
porcelain were found at Wormslow.

All deposits, except those dating after circa 1790, contained
sherds of plain, sand-tempered Colono-Indian pottery. Most
of the fragments were plain body sherds and therefore vessel
shapes could not be determined. However, a large section of
what appears to be the rim from a deep dish or pan made of
Colono-Indian pottery was found (see fig. 52, no. 17). This
piece was apparently decorated with rim notching in an attempt to copy Staffordshire notched-rim slipware dishes
which were also used and discarded at the site.

Glass

Fragments of at least 177 wine bottles were recovered, the
shapes ranging in date from about 1725 to 1800 (see fig. 50).
The bulk of the bottles were found in pit A (deposited ca.
1737–1740), pit B (ca. 1750–1760) and pit C (ca. 1770–
1790). It is interesting to note that one particular style,
manufactured in the approximate period of 1735 to 1760,
was the predominant type found in all three deposits, even
in association with artifacts dating after 1770 (see fig. 41).
As a whole, the bottles from the site vividly reflect the notion
that wine bottles of the eighteenth century evolved from the
squat "onion" shape in earlier years to the "modern" cylindrical shape by the end of the colonial period. One bottle was
found completely intact. It had a capacity of exactly four-
fifths of a quart, suggesting that the modern liquor unit of
measure, a "fifth," goes back to the eighteenth century.

At least five square sectioned "case gin" bottles were found,
displaying three entirely different string rims. The rim forms
apparently had nothing to do with the date of their manufacture. One pale green square sectioned bottle was also
found, apparently of French manufacture. Several pale green

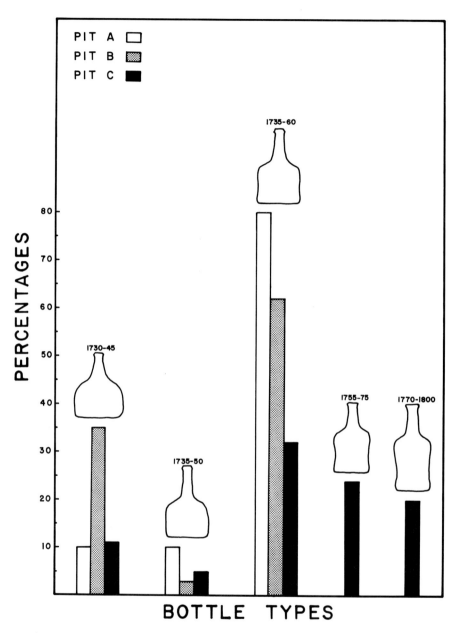

Fig. 41. The percentage of particular wine bottle styles recovered in each of three deposits: pits A, B, and C.

glass pharmaceutical bottles were also recovered (see fig. 51, nos. 8–13).

A few drinking glasses were found (see fig. 51, nos. 1–7). Wineglasses were generally plain stemmed with a trumpet bowl, typical of the mid–eighteenth century. Two of the wineglass stems were ornamented with teardrops. Fragments of a large engraved drinking glass or "rummer" were found in the well fill (deposited ca. 1770–1790).

Tools

The root-infested sandy soil of the Georgia coast would not yield to standard plowing at first; thus the newly cleared lands had to be laboriously tilled by hand hoeing. It is not surprising therefore that a total of nine broad and narrow iron hoes were found on the site (see fig. 55). One broad hoe may have had a maker's mark stamped on it, but the impression is unreadable. A large felling axe and a small hatchet were recovered from the well; the axe was stamped with a heart-shaped maker's mark. Two square-blade spades came from the well fill, both made of sheet iron. The smaller hand tools recovered included a pair of iron pinchers possibly marked with the initial *L*, two half-round and two triangular files, three "gimblets" or hand drills, one regular wood drill, two carpenter's dividers, and a fragment of a sawblade (see fig. 56).

Household Implements and Hardware

Three identical three-pound flatirons were found. They presumably had had thin iron handles which did not survive (see figs. 42 and 55). One pair of iron scissors was also found, which had probably been used either for cutting cloth or for barbering. Two brass thimbles and several straight pins were found at the same level, near the back door of the kitchen. The thimbles were made in two pieces with wall sections brazed to the crowns. The indentations on the side

Fig. 42. Scissors, brass thimbles, pins, and a three-pound flatiron.

walls are round but become square on the crown, giving them a crosshatched appearance. The largest thimble measures 15 mm at the opening and 19 mm in height, while the smallest, probably for a child's sampler work, measures 11 mm at the opening and 13 mm high. The straight pins were made of tin-plated brass with handmade knotted heads.

Cutlery and Spoons

A fair sampling of cutlery and spoons was recovered at Wormslow (see fig. 52, nos. 1–13). Some table knives had two-piece bone handles and most of the blades were typical of the mid–eighteenth century. Two clasp knives with pistol grip handles were also found. The one fork recovered had a two-piece pistol-grip bone handle and two tines. Spoons of latten (tin-plated brass), pewter, and iron were found. Both the latten and pewter spoon bowls had rat-tail reinforcing spines along the underside, and both had been well worn on the same side, probably the result of continued use by a right-handed person.

Iron Hardware

Portions of several "T" and "HL" iron hinges and four iron pintles were found at the site (see fig. 58), the former two types matching a purchase made by Noble Jones at Rasberry's store in 1759. The smaller pintles were no doubt for shutter hinges. Four iron hooks were also found. One had a rectangular hole through the shank, probably made to take a wedge-shaped securing key. Another hook with a thin flat shank must have been wedged in a mortar joint, perhaps over the hearth, and two iron "eye" hooks were also found, one still having fragments of chain attached to it. An iron key and four locks were found (see fig. 56, nos. 12–16). The key was hollow at the end of the shank and made to fit locks with iron post key guides. Two locks with post-key guides were also found at Wormslow, one probably from a drawer and the other for a door. One plate "stock lock," typical of the late eighteenth and early nineteenth centuries, was also recovered along with a bag-shaped padlock. Noble Jones also bought stock locks and padlocks from Rasberry's store in 1760

Barn and Stable Equipment

Iron pieces from at least one and probably two saddles were found in the well (deposited ca. 1770–1790) (see fig. 57). The cantle (rear seat) piece and front cleat from the saddle-tree are commonly found on eighteenth-century sites, but an iron "horn" pommel was also recovered, which is surprising in such an early context. A curb bit, completely intact, was also found along with two cowbells. The bells were made of sheet brass alloy riveted along one side. The smaller rectangular type is common, having been made continually from medieval times to the present day. However, the larger of the two was unusual in that the shoulders were wider than the mouth, which may be strictly an eighteenth-century characteristic.

Buckles

Various types of buckles were found, the bulk of which had been used on either shoes or harnesses (see fig. 51, nos. 15–41). A rounded brass and an intricately wrought iron shoe buckle were also found. Both brass and iron harness buckles of various sizes were recovered.

Buttons and Miscellaneous Brass

A representative collection of eighteenth-century buttons made of glass, bone, pewter, brass, or brass and bone were found at Wormslow (see fig. 54). Bone and brass buttons with four fastener holes and plain turned brass types with soldered loop fasteners were common. One large engraved button was also found, as well as a tin-plated brass example. Other items of brass included a brass candlestick with height adjuster in the shank made of iron and lead, a beaded sheet brass candlestick drip pan, and an engraved "dragon" side-plate from an "Indian trade" type of musket, marked with a crown over the initials *IW* (probably made by John Whatley in London in the 1770s).

Gunflints and Spalls

A total of eighteen gunflints and spalls were found on the site (see fig. 53), and enough "black" flint nodules and worked chips to indicate that the occupants were attempting gunflint manufacturing. However, twelve of the eighteen flints and spalls were made of honey-colored brown type of flint usually attributed to French origin. No nodules or chips of this type of flint were found.

Coins

The only specifically datable artifacts found on the site were two English coins, one a farthing dated 1754. It is possible that this coin is counterfeit in that the E in REX is poorly stamped and the dot is missing after the Roman numeral II (see fig. 43).[1] It was found inside the house, along the central

Fig. 43. Obverse and reverse of an English copper farthing, 1754, found in the kitchen of the main building.

tabby partition, and although it was lying at the same level as the top of the yellow sand subfloor of the building, it could have fallen through the crack between the floor material (tile) and the partition wall. The other coin, an extremely worn George III halfpenny of 1772 or 1775 (date was unreadable), was found between the tabby floor blocks in the southwest room and had obviously fallen through a crack in the floor. Neither coin was found in a level helpful to date the building, but they give more credence to the range of dates of the occupation.

Miscellaneous Finds

Three musket balls (33D, 5G, 4F) were found, ranging in size from 51 to 62 caliber. Fishing weights, apparently made from musket balls (1B, 3C, 2F), were also found, as well as a cast triangular net sinker and an iron fishhook, 25 mm in length (15B). Two marbles (18A, 24A) were also recovered, one made of clay and the other actually made of marble (20 mm in diameter).

A large roughly conical fifty-pound lead weight with an iron eye was found (see fig. 44). Unfortunately it was found in a disturbed area just east of and entangled in the roots of the cedar tree that now grows on the partition wall between rooms 4 and 5 of the house. No datable artifacts were found with the piece. Three large grooves, appearing as though they had been made by blows from an axe, were cut into the upper face of the weight. The purpose of such a heavy piece is uncertain, but it may have been used as a counterweight for the main curtain gate.

Building Materials

Fragments of building materials were found throughout the site, but they were not concentrated at any one level, with the exception of oyster shells and mortar spill along the house and enclosure walls. In addition to tabby and nails of

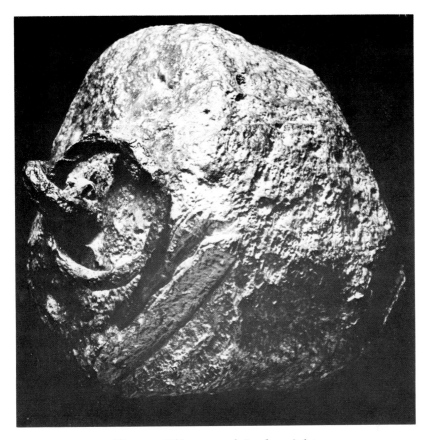

Fig. 44. Fifty-pound lead weight.

various sizes, two types of brick and two types of plaster were recovered. Rectangular bricks and brickbats were found, generally measuring $3\frac{1}{4}'' \times 4'' \times 2\frac{3}{8}''$, of either red or orange color and containing flecks of dark gray impurities fired to a cinderlike appearance. The other type of brick (compass bricks used in the well) measured $8\frac{1}{2}'' \times 5'' \times 3'' \times 2\frac{3}{8}''$ and had an entirely different body consisting of orange clay streaked with ocher. In effect the body of the well brick appears marbled, almost in the manner of the body of some English slipware. The rectangular bricks are generally the same size as the English bricks used at Frederica, although bricks of the same size were being locally made there as early as 1741 by Captain Mark Carr. It could be that Noble Jones on his frequent runs to Frederica returned with bricks made by Carr. On the other hand, compass-shaped well bricks were unusual in Georgia. No wedge-shaped bricks were used in the numerous wells at Frederica, and it was not until March 1744 that "new bricks [were] formed in a proper mould to make the work [well] Circular."[2]

Both types of plaster found at the site were made of oyster-shell mortar faced with a thin layer of fine white mortar (see fig. 45). Some of the fragments retain regular flat lathe marks, probably having faced wooden partition walls and ceiling. However, a considerable quantity of plaster with oyster-shell

Fig. 45. Examples of wattle and daub mortar (upper left), lath plaster (upper right), mortar and brick plug from tabby construction (lower left), and a fragment of plaster apparently inscribed with the letters *NJone*.

chips in it and half-round impressions on one side, presumably formed by the saplings from wattle and daub construction, were found. One piece of this daubing seems to have had letters inscribed on it. In some light they appear to be *NJone,* but this may or may not be the actual inscription (see fig. 45, lower right). At any rate, one of these pieces with the round impressions was found under the tabby wall of the house, suggesting that earlier wattle and daub construction existed at the site before the tabby work. One other fragment of building material is worthy of mention. A cylindrical piece of mortar with a fragment of brick at one end was found in pit E (ca. 1800–1820) along with discarded loose tabby (see fig. 45, lower right). The cylinder is the right diameter to have been one of the mortar and brick plugs used to fill the form peg holes in the tabby walls. This piece with the tabby heap suggests that pit E was in fact dug during a repair job, probably during work done on the enclosure wall located a few feet to the east. Finally, corner fragments of square (?) orange brick floor tiles, 3/4″ thick, were found in the well, the only other evidence (besides the mortar impressions) of the existence of a brick tile floor in room 1.

Nails ranging from 3/4″ to 5″ in length were found throughout the site (see fig. 58, nos. 31 and 32). All were hand wrought and rectangular in section with rose-pointed heads.

Animal and Marine Remains

A considerable number of bones and shells were found during the course of the excavations. Enough identifiable remains were found in pit A, pit C, and pit E to give some insight into the diet of the Wormslow inhabitants. The collection was analyzed by William R. Adams, Department of Anthropology, University of Indiana, Bloomington, who submitted the following report:

Pit A contains a fairly large number of deer bones (*Odocoileus virginianus*) which, on analysis, show that at least three indi-

viduals were involved. The second most numerous species was
Bos taurus (domestic cattle) and here again it would appear that
at least two individuals were represented. The domestic swine
(*Sus scrofa*) was represented in smaller quantity. Other species
represented, but in small quantities, were the opossum (*Didelphus virginianus*), the domestic chicken (*Gallus domesticus*),
one or more species of marine crab, one oyster (*Ostrea equestris*)
(*Say*), one raccoon (*Procyon lotor*), one hooded merganser
(*Lophodytes cucullatus*), one bird which is probably the sand
hill crane (*Grus canadensis*), and one bone which represents
either domestic sheep or goats.

Pit C had the largest assortment of bones—a large number of
which were that of domestic chicken (*Gallus domesticus*). Fifty-
two specimens were present which represented the skeleton of a
young individual. There were ten bones of a second young individual and twenty-seven of yet another individual. A total of
ninety-three bones of this species were present. In every case
these were bones of young individuals being relatively intact and
with no evidence of cutting or chewing. The common rat (*Rattus
norvegicus*) was evident from this pit with a total of thirty-five
bones, thirty-one apparently belonging to one individual. A
rather large number of bones of frog (*Rana*) were in evidence
and these appear to be of the species *pipiens*—the common leop-
ard frog. One, however, was identified as *Rana catesbiana*—the
bull frog. Again a number of fragments of marine crab pinchers
were in evidence and bones of cattle (*Bos taurus*) and swine
(*Sus scrofa*). A number of shell fragments were present. These
were small and it is not known whether they may be egg shells or
perhaps crustacean shells. Also present in limited numbers were
Virginia deer (*Odocoileus virginianus*), bobwhite quail (*Colinus
virginianus*), a number of bones of the *Ictaluridae* (the catfishes),
two of a fish probably belonging to the *Centrarchidae* and some
unidentified fish bones and fish scales. Also, there was an unidentified bird bone. There was one carapace fragment of an
unidentified species of turtle, two bones of the groundhog (*Mar-
mota monax*), and five bones of the dog (*Canis familiaris*), and
one of a bobcat of *Lynx rufus*.

As for pit E, we again find cattle (*Bos taurus*) which could represent one or more than one individual. The remains of the swine (*Sus scrofa*) indicate that at least three individuals are represented—and perhaps more. Bones present of the Virginia deer (*Odocoileus virginianus*) would indicate that at least two individuals are represented. In the case of the raccoon (*Procyon lotor*) the six bones found in pit E appear to have come from one individual. This area also yielded one oppossum bone (*Didelphus virginianus*), one sheep or goat bone and the shell of a marine mollusk (*Andara ovalis*) (*Bruguiere*), as well as fourteen claw fragments of a marine crustacean.[3]

CONCLUSION

The artifact collection from the Wormslow excavations provides a specific look at the types of items used on a small eighteenth-century coastal Georgia plantation. The quality of the artifacts, as a whole, does not reflect great wealth when compared to those found on the vast self-sufficient plantations of other colonies. The artifacts (as well as the architecture) suggest that Wormslow was a summer retreat for the wealthy and politically active Jones family, rather than their primary residence. A more complete assessment of the taste and economic well-being of the eighteenth-century Jones family would have to come from an archaeological study of their numerous, more permanent homes in Savannah, a project rendered difficult, if not impossible, by subsequent urban development.

More importantly, the artifact collection is the only assemblage of items used in the eighteenth-century Savannah area to have been gathered archaeologically. With the Wormslow articles in hand, Georgia historical documents such as merchants' orders and bills, wills, inventories, account books, and descriptions take on new meaning. For example the Wormslow artifacts can help define more exactly what the Savannah merchant Thomas Rasberry meant when he ordered "white stone plates" from London in 1759 or billed Noble Jones for a "stock lock" in 1760.[4] And it is hoped that the collection will serve as a gauge to measure similar collections from future archaeological studies of eighteenth-century sites in coastal Georgia.

Finally, beyond showing that the occupants of Wormslow typically relied on British-made articles, the artifacts specifically suggest that: (1) a pottery that made lead-glazed coarse earthenware probably existed in the Savannah area; (2) someone (probably Indians) was making pottery vessels of local clay in an attempt to copy English slipware forms; (3) the hoe was a vital tool for small Georgia coastal plantations, as the documents suggest; (4) the occupants of Wormslow attempted to manufacture some of their own gunflints and spalls.

Artifact Illustrations

INTRODUCTION

Artifacts deemed representative and significant found at Wormslow are illustrated and described on the following pages. The descriptions following each illustration page will generally follow this form: item number, type of object, place of manufacture, material from which the object was made, description of salient features, date of manufacture, number of the trench and letter of the layer within which the object was found (i.e., its excavation register number), and finally the catalogue number prefixed by the letter *W*. Artifacts recovered from any of the five major trash pits found on the site are so noted. The probable deposition dates are:

Pit A	1737–1740
Pit B	1750–1760
Pit C	1770–1790
Pit D	1785– ?
Pit E	1790–1820

It should be pointed out that the *terminus post quem* dates of the various Wormslow features are based upon the earliest manufacturing date of the most recent artifact found in each deposit and that the terminal dates for the deposits are based on the probable popularity span of that given artifact type. Therefore in some cases the manufacturing date span included in the descriptions below may run earlier or later than the deposit date.

All reconstructed drawings are based on either similar or

identical illustrated pieces or on a logical projection of the missing pieces.

Appendix A includes a list, description, and probable deposit date of the layers of stratigraphy within which the illustrated artifacts were found.

Coarse Earthenware
Figure 46

1. Small pot, coarse earthenware, beige body covered with a thick drab green glaze, scrolled handle terminal, base unglazed but orange in color.[1] Pit C. (30B, C) W/12

2. Storage jar base, coarse earthenware, slightly domed base, red body fired black near outer edge, maroon lead glazing on exterior, interior and base unglazed. Pit C. (30E) W/13

3. Small shallow jar or storage jar cover, coarse earthenware, beige body fired orange red at surface, rim has V-shaped groove along top to provide for tight fit, thin lip, slightly domed base. Pit C. (30E) W/14

4. Storage jar or pan rim fragment, coarse earthenware, beige body covered with yellow glaze inside, two perforations (3 mm diameter) below rim made before firing (the glaze seeped through both), holes possibly for thong handle, folded and thickened rim. Pit C. (32C) W/15

5. Cream pan rim fragment, coarse earthenware, beige body covered with mottled brown and green lead glaze on exterior, pinched spout mark at one end, interior fired orange in color. Pit C. (30H) W/16

6. Cream pan rim fragment, coarse earthenware, beige body covered with a mottled salmon glaze on interior, rolled rim.[2] Pit C. (30E) W/17

7. Cream pan rim fragment, coarse earthenware, beige body covered with a mottled salmon and green lead glaze, folded rim rounded on the edges. (33B) W/18

8. Cream pan rim fragment, coarse earthenware, red body covered with a chocolate brown lead glaze on interior. (32A) W/19

9. Cream pan rim sherd, coarse earthenware, pink body cov-

ered with a drab brown mottled glaze, folded rim with narrowed edge similar to no. 18 below. Pit C. (30K) W/20

10. Cream pan rim fragment and spout, coarse earthenware, beige body covered with a mottled grayish brown lead glaze on the exterior. (32B) W/21

11. Jar rim fragment, coarse earthenware, red body covered with a mottled salmon glaze, everted rim. Pit C. (30K) W/22

12. Bowl rim and base fragment, coarse earthenware, red body covered with a caramel brown glaze on interior, splashes of glaze on exterior, diameter of base conjectural, slightly rolled rim with V-shaped groove around vessel 15 mm below rim. Pit C. (30K) W/23

13. Jug or bottle neck fragment, coarse earthenware, pink unglazed body, fine potting rings on interior and exterior, ridge below upper fracture possibly simulating a string rim.[3] (33B) W/24

14. Large storage jar or jug base fragment, coarse earthenware, pink unglazed earthenware as no. 13 above, deep potting rings on interior, slightly domed base, heavy thick walls and base diameter suggest that the vessel must have been extremely large. (17C) W/25

15. Cream pan rim and base corner fragment, coarse earthenware, slightly pink body, folded rim, caramel brown glaze on interior, thumb-pinched spout, exterior unglazed and fired to a salmon color, size conjectural. Pit C. (30E) W/26

16. Cream pan rim and base fragment, same ware as no. 15 above, exterior unglazed, body color slightly darkened by firing, size conjectural. Pit C. (30E) W/27

17. Cream pan rim and base corner fragment, slightly pink body covered with a mottled honey-colored glaze, glaze chipped off on exterior. Pit A. (7E[4]) W/28

18. Cream pan rim and base fragment, coarse earthenware, pink body covered with a greenish brown lead glaze on the interior and splashes of dark brown lead glaze on the exterior, folded rim form identical to no. 9 above, slightly domed base. (1B) W/29

19. Cream pan or bowl rim and base sherds, coarse earthenware, pink body covered with a caramel brown lead glaze, much thinner than above examples, folded rim, slightly domed base. (15F) W/30

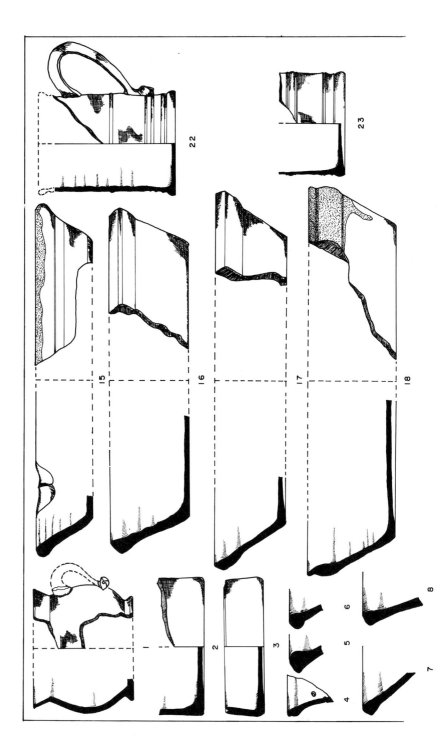

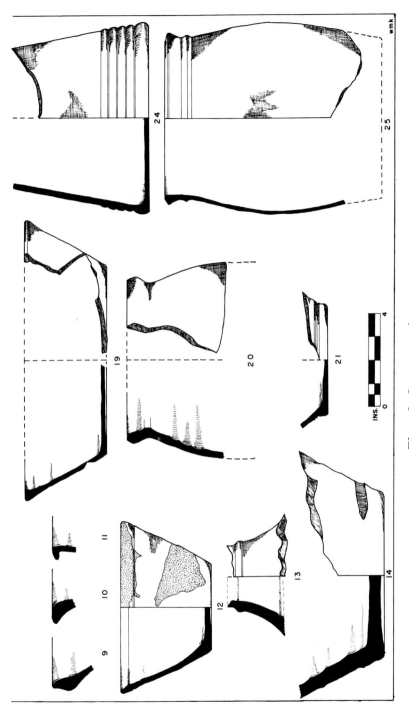

Fig. 46. Coarse earthenware.

20. Storage jar rim fragment, coarse earthenware, beige body covered with an orange glaze on the interior, exterior fired orange, everted rim with inner ridge probably made to take a lid. Pit C. (32C) W/31

21. Storage jar base (?), coarse earthenware, beige body covered with a honey brown glaze, grooved around exterior just above base. Pit C. (30E) W/32

22. Mug, coarse earthenware, possibly made at Bethabara, North Carolina by Rudolph Christ (1770–1800), light beige body covered with a mottled red and green glaze on the exterior and a drab green glaze on the interior; glaze was allowed to build up as much as $\frac{1}{8}''$ on one side of interior base, potting rings plainly visible on interior, exterior banded in the pewter manner, triangular handle terminal, handle saddle-shaped in section, last quarter of the eighteenth century.[4] Pit C. (30E) W/33

23. Mug base fragment, coarse earthenware, pink body covered with a drab green lead glaze on the exterior, olive green glaze on the interior, grooved in the same manner as no. 22 above (presumably to imitate pewter or silver), not the same ware as above, domed base. Pit C. (30E) W/34

24. Pitcher or storage jar base, coarse earthenware, beige body covered with a honey-colored slip on the interior, part of what appears to be an incised number 4 on body 4″ above the base (presumably marking capacity), sides pronouncedly in-sloping suggesting that this vessel was a pitcher, base and one side blackened by fire. Pit C. (32C) W/35

25. Storage jar rim and body fragment, coarse earthenware, beige to slightly pinkish body covered with a maroon glaze on interior, exterior fired to a mottled orange and purple color. Pit A. (7E ²) W/36

Stoneware, Chinese Porcelain, Delftware, and Slipware
Figure 47

1. Bellarmine bottle (?), Rhenish stoneware, light salmon to tan body, mottled brown glaze, no trace of usual mask since opposite side broken off (therefore it may or may not have had one), first quarter eighteenth century.[5] Pit C. (30J) W/37

2. Chamberpot, gray Westerwald stoneware, rim and handle

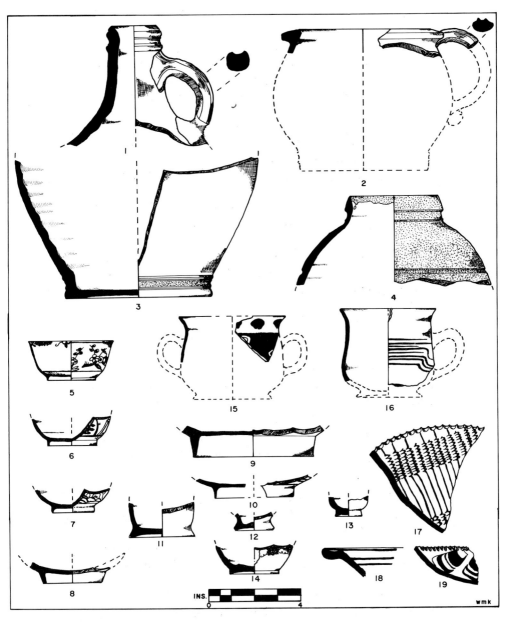

Fig. 47. German stoneware, English stoneware, Chinese porcelain,
English porcelain, delftware, and slipware.

fragment only, tracts of cobalt blue band below rim, 1720–1760.[6] (31A) W/36

3. Pitcher or storage jar base, gray Westerwald stoneware, band of lightly applied cobalt blue above base, exterior glaze shows slight traces of mottled light brown on the gray body, trace of cobalt blue medallion (?) on middle of body, 1720–1760.[7] Pit B. (14C) W/39

4. Storage jar, English saltglazed stoneware (?), beige body fired to salmon color on interior, deep maroon-colored exterior glaze, fine potting rings on interior. (9D) W/40

5. Cup, Chinese porcelain, decorated in underglaze blue showing simple floral and pastoral scenes on exterior, leaf and scroll-like pattern along interior rim, single blue line along base of interior wall, reconstructed from fragments, eighteenth century.[8] (31 B,E,M) W/41

6. Cup fragment, Chinese porcelain, decorated in underglaze blue as no. 5 above, heavy footring, simple stick tree and floral design, single blue line along base of interior wall, eighteenth century. (18B) W/42

7. Cup fragment, English porcelain, decorated in dark underglaze blue showing simple floral design, trace of sticklike mark on interior of base, heavy footring. Pit E. (20B) W/43

8. Bowl, Chinese porcelain, decorated in underglaze blue as no. 5 above, heavy incurving footring, center of interior base marked with three leaves, eighteenth century.[9] Pit C. (30H) W/44

9. Punch bowl base, English delftware, tin enameled glaze slightly blue, heavy footring slightly in-tapering. Judging by base diameter and thickness of walls, the vessel must have been quite large, possibly 12″ to 14″ in diameter at the rim, eighteenth century. Pit C. (30M) W/45

10. Basin base fragment, English delftware, white glaze with hint of pink, V-shaped footring, decorated in cobalt blue rings on interior and exterior, eighteenth century.[10] (31H) W/46

11. Drug jar, English delftware, pinkish white glaze suggests Lambeth for the place of manufacture, eighteenth century.[11] (6H) W/47

12. Pharmaceutical ointment-pot, English delftware, bluish white glaze, domed base, eighteenth century.[12] (2K) W/48

13. Pharmaceutical ointment-pot base, English delftware, bluish white glaze as no. 12 above, smaller base, distinct wire marks

on base where vessel was cut on wheel, eighteenth century. (5L) W/49

14. Cup base or drug jar fragment, English delftware, bluish white glaze as above, decorated in cobalt blue hand-painted floral designs, a body fragment found in the same level shows a cherub which probably was part of the motif, interior undecorated, early eighteenth century.[13] (5E) W/50

15. Posset cup rim fragment, Staffordshire or Bristol slipware, decorated in dark brown on a cream yellow background, conjectural shape based on an intact example with identical decoration, outflaring rim, bulbous body, late seventeenth or first half of the eighteenth century.[14] Pit E. (20C) W/51

16. Posset cup, Staffordshire slipware, pale yellow bulbous body, outflaring rim, dark brown body combing, conjectural shape based on similar decorated example dated 1735, first half of the eighteenth century.[15] Pit C. (30E) W/52

17. Dish rim fragment, Staffordshire slipware, notched rim, salmon body streaked with brown, pale yellow glaze, combed design, first half of the eighteenth century.[16] Pit C. (32C) W/53

18. Bowl rim fragment, slipware, rust-colored body decorated with trails of yellow slip, eighteenth century. Pit C. (30K) W/54

19. Dish, Staffordshire slipware, notched rim, same ware and decorative technique as no. 17 above, second quarter of the eighteenth century.[17] Pit C. (30K) W/55

English White Saltglazed Stoneware, Creamware, and Pearlware
Figure 48

1. Cup, English white saltglazed stoneware, slight outflaring rim beveled along interior, traditional orange-skin texture, extremely thin but not translucent, 1740–1770.[18] Pit C. (30E) W/65

2. Cup, English white saltglazed stoneware, same as no. 1 above with the exception of a squared-off thinner footring, 1740–1770. Pit C. (30M,L,K) W/66

3. Saucer, English (probably Staffordshire) white saltglazed stoneware, body has a slightly grayish blue hue when compared with no. 1 and no. 2 above, decorated in scratch blue floral and leaf designs, chevron rouletting around interior base, slight outflaring rim, 1750–1775.[19] Pit C. (32C 30G) W/67

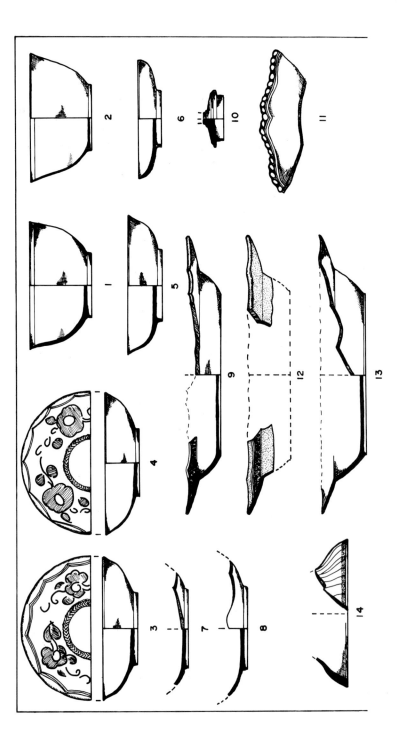

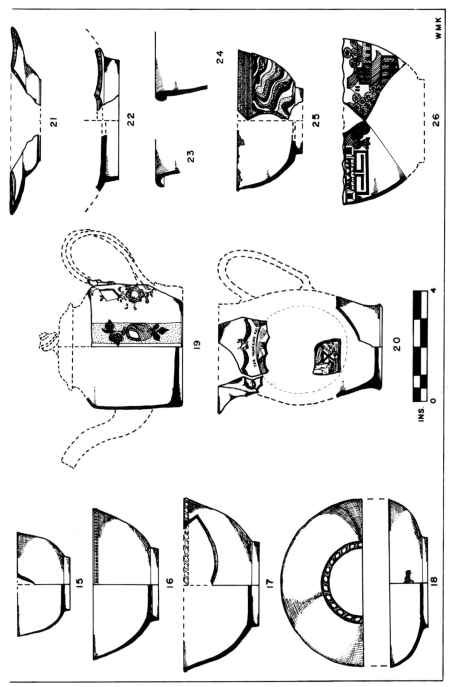

Fig. 48. English white saltglazed stoneware, creamware, and pearlware.

4. Saucer, English white saltglazed stoneware, probably Staffordshire, identical with no. 3 above with the exception that the design was probably applied by another artist since the flowers are more circular, all pieces of this vessel were recovered, 1750–1775. Pit C. (30E 32C) W/68

5. Saucer, English white saltglazed stoneware, same ware as no. 1 and no. 2 above, slight outflaring rim, heavy footring, 1740–1770. Pit C. (30E) W/69

6. Small saucer, English white saltglazed stoneware, drab white compared with no. 5 above, thick body, both characteristics suggesting an earlier date than the above examples, 1740–1760. (31J) W/70

7. Saucer base fragment, English white saltglazed stoneware, same ware as no. 5 above with less orange-skin appearance, 1740–1770. Pit C. (32C) W/71

8. Saucer base fragment, English white saltglazed stoneware, same ware as no. 5 above, slightly beveled footring, 1740–1770. Pit C. (30E) W/72

9. Plate, English white saltglazed stoneware, rim molded with dot, diaper, and basket pattern, slightly domed base with trace of a footring, 1740–1760.[20] Pit C. (12C) W/73

10. Teapot lid, English white saltglazed stoneware, knob broken off, same ware as no. 6 above, 1740–1770.[21] (31L) W/74

11. Plate rim fragment, English white saltglazed stoneware, same ware as no. 9 above, bead and reel molded border decoration, 1750–1775.[22] Pit C. (32C) W/75

12. Plate rim fragment, English green creamware, molded barley pattern around rim, 1759–1775.[23] Pit C. (30M) W/76

13. Plate fragment, English creamware, deep bowl, slight footring, rim in the Royal Pattern, 1765–?[24] Pit D. (12C) W/77

14. Vase or sugar bowl lid (?), English creamware, edged in green, glaze has a distinct greenish hue, exterior fluted, rim flattened, 1770–?[25] (16C) W/78

15. Cup, English creamware, light cream finish, highly glossy, sherd approximately one-third of whole vessel (therefore it may have had a handle), thin walled, 1765–? Pit C. (30F) W/79

16. Cup, English creamware, beaded rim molding, V-shaped footring, deep yellow color, handleless, 1765–1785 (?).[26] Pit C. (30K,L) W/80

17. Cup, English creamware, bead and reel or rope molded rim

design, V-shaped footring, deep yellow glaze as above, 1765–1785 (?). (27B) W/81

18. Saucer, English creamware, bead and reel or rope molded design as no. 17 above, same deep yellow glaze as no. 16 and no. 17 above, 1765–1785. Pit C. (30K) W/82

19. Teapot body fragment, English creamware, probably Leeds, hand painted in overglaze purple, crimson and green, light cream finish as no. 15 above, floral terminal shows evidence of double intertwined handle, conjectural shape based on identical hand-painted example dated 1775.[27] Pit E. (20C) W/83

20. Jug; English creamware; usually referred to as a "Liverpool Jug;" spout, rim, and body fragments only; light cream color as no. 15 and no. 19 above; transfer-printed in black with "The Wand'ring Sai[lor]" scene on side panel with an anchor and drape border design, scene apparently showed a standing sailor behind a seated sailor in striped pants with a sitting dog at his feet, both in front of a building with a sailing ship sign hanging from the roof (presumably a tavern), title suggests a verse from a song "the Wand'ring Sailor;" 1790–1810.[28] (20C, 9B, 3C, 3A) W/84

21. Plate rim and footring fragment, English creamware, light cream finish as nos. 15, 19, and 20 above, Queen's shape rim molding, shallow footring, 1765–?. Pit E. (20B) W/85

22. Bowl or basin base fragment, English creamware, deep thick footring, light cream glaze, 1765–?. (32A) W/86

23. Bowl or basin rim fragment, English creamware, light cream color as above, possibly from same vessel, everted rim, 1765–?. (31A) W/87

24. Bowl or basin rim fragment, English creamware, light cream glaze, rolled rim, late eighteenth–early nineteenth century.[29] Pit E. (20C) W/88

25. Cup, English creamware, rim decorated with small engine-turned grooves filled with dark green, body decorated with polychrome (white, beige, light blue, tan, and dark brown) marbling, usual yellowish green glaze buildup in footring corners, 1785–1815.[30] (2D) W/89

26. Bowl rim fragment, English pearlware, transfer-printed in cobalt blue with a Chinese architectural scene on the exterior and the traditional willow pattern border design on the interior, late eighteenth–early nineteenth century.[31] (2D) W/90

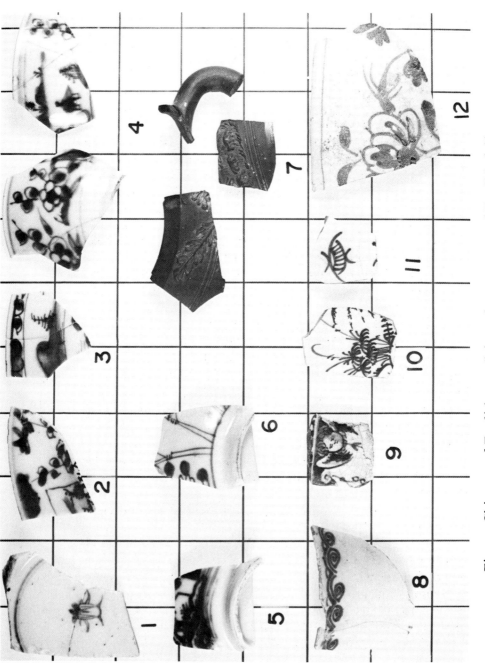

Fig. 49. Chinese and English porcelain, red stoneware, and English delftware.

Chinese and English Porcelain, Red Stoneware,
and English Delftware
Figure 49

1. Bowl or cup base, Chinese porcelain, decorated in underglaze blue and marked with a pair of fish over a knot (the Buddhist symbol for happiness in marriage) darker underglaze blue design on opposite side, eighteenth century.[32] Pit C. (30D) W/56

2. Saucer rim fragment, Chinese porcelain, underglaze blue floral decoration on interior, eighteenth century. (31A) (Similar design fig. 43, no. 5). W/57

3. Cup rim fragment, Chinese porcelain, decorated in underglaze blue pattern on exterior, single blue line along interior of rim, eighteenth century. Pit C. W/58

4. Cup, Chinese porcelain, eighteenth century. (31B, E, M) (See fig. 43, no. 5 above).

5. Cup rim fragment, English porcelain, body much whiter and glaze more glossy than nos. 1–4 above, deep cobalt blue underglaze leaf decoration, heavy rounded footring, second half of the eighteenth century. Pit E. (20B) (See fig. 43, no. 7 above).

6. Cup base fragment, Chinese porcelain, underglaze blue tree and leaf design, eighteenth century (18B) (See fig. 43, no. 6 above).

7. Small teapot fragments, English dry-body red stoneware, molded sprigged decoration consisting of foliate motif and small animals (horses?), small loop handle round in section, top of wall grooved for lid, extremely thin walled, third quarter of the eighteenth century.[33] Pit B. (14B) W/59

8. Mug or base rim fragment, English delftware, decorated in cobalt blue scroll-circles around outside rim, lip worn through the glaze, second half of the eighteenth century.[34] Pit D. (12C) W/60

9. Bowl or cup body fragment, English delftware, early eighteenth century. (5E) (Possibly part of a vessel shown in fig. 43, no. 14 above). W/61

10. Bowl rim fragment, English delftware, chinoiserie floral and tree design in cobalt blue on the exterior. Pit C. (30E) W/62

11. Bowl body fragment, English delftware, Chinese symbol (?) in cobalt blue on exterior. Pit E. (20C) W/63

12. Bowl rim fragment, English delftware, Bristol (?), decorated in cobalt blue floral pattern with portions of the flower petals done in overglaze red-orange, single line along rim, eighteenth century.[35] Pit C. (30E) W/64

Wine Bottles
Figure 50

1. Wine bottle, amber-green glass, V-shaped string rim, wide conical basal kick, glass completely undecayed, 90 percent restored from fragments, 1730–1745.[36] Pit A. (7E⁴) W/91

2. Wine bottle, olive green glass, V-shaped string rim, domed basal kick, 90 percent restored from fragments, 1735–1750.[37] Pit A. (7E³) W/92

3. Wine bottle, olive green glass, V-shaped string rim, neck much thicker and mouth wider in diameter than no. 1 and no. 2 above, deep conical kick, body sagged near base, probably a "roughly" made variety of the style illustrated in no. 1 above, 1730–1745. Pit E. (20G) W/93

4. Wine bottle, olive green glass, down tooled string rim, conical basal kick, shoulders wider than base, 90 percent restored from fragments, 1735–1760. Pit A. (7E³) W/94

5. Wine bottle, olive green glass, double ridged string rim tooled flat parallel to body, domed basal kick, shoulders wider than base, sides slightly concave from sagging, completely intact (capacity 25 ounces: 4/5 of a quart), 1755–1775. Pit C. (30G) W/95

6. Wine bottle, olive green glass, double ridged string rim flattened as no. 5 above, deep domed basal kick, neck could not be joined to body but color and context suggest that both pieces came from same bottle, 1755–1775. Pit C. (30K) W/96

7. Wine bottle, light green glass, mouth everted over a down tooled string rim, deep conical basal kick, wider at shoulder than at base, concave sides, neck and base could not be joined but color and context suggest that they came from the same bottle, 1770–1800. Pit C. (30M) W/97

8. Wine bottle neck, olive green glass, V-shaped string rim thick sides, 1725–1735. Pit B. (14B) W/98

9. Wine bottle neck, light green glass, everted mouth over a heavy V-shaped string rim, sides bulged out below string rim, 1725–1735?. Pit B. (14B) W/99

10. Wine bottle neck, dark olive green glass, mouth slightly everted over V-shaped string rim, 1725–1745. Pit B. (14B) W/100

11. Wine bottle neck, olive green glass, heavy V-shaped string rim, probably from same bottle type as no. 1 above, found sealed beneath tabby partition foundation in house, 1730–1745. (24E) W/101

12. Wine bottle neck, olive green glass, everted mouth over V-shaped string rim, sharply spreading shoulder suggests a body shape similar to no. 4 above, 1740–1760. Pit B. (14B) W/102

13. Wine bottle neck, light green glass, heavily corroded, sharply everted mouth over a heavy V-shaped string rim shoulders spread as no. 4 and no. 12 above, 1740–1760. Pit B. (14B) W/103

14. Wine bottle neck, amber green glass, down tooled string rim, rounded shoulders, 1770–1800 (?).[38] Pit C. (30P) W/104

15. Wine bottle neck, light olive green glass, mouth thickened and down tooled over a flattened string rim, neck slightly bulbous, 1770–1800. Pit D. (12C) W/105

16. Wine bottle neck, olive green glass, wide everted mouth down tooled over flattened string rim as no. 15 above, but sides more bulbous and neck longer, 1770–1800. Pit C. (30F) W/106

17. Wine bottle base, light green glass, heavily corroded, slightly sagging body, domed basal kick, 1790–1810. (2J) W/107

18. Bottle, French (?), pale blue-green glass, body square in section, slightly everted struck mouth, thin walled, mid-eighteenth century. Pit C. (30K) W/108

19. Case bottle neck, olive green glass, thick everted mouth. (31L) W/109

20. Case bottle base and neck, light green glass heavily corroded, everted mouth above a rolled string rim, body square in section, heavy pontil scar on under base, body in-tapering, side panels slightly concave, height conjectural, eighteenth century.[39] Pit B. (14B) W/110

21. Case bottle, neck and base, light green glass, everted mouth, string rim rounded and up tooled slightly, longer neck than no. 19 and no. 20 above, shoulders considerably wider than base, broad conical basal kick, rough pontil scar, height conjectural, eighteenth century.[40] Pit B. (14B) W/111

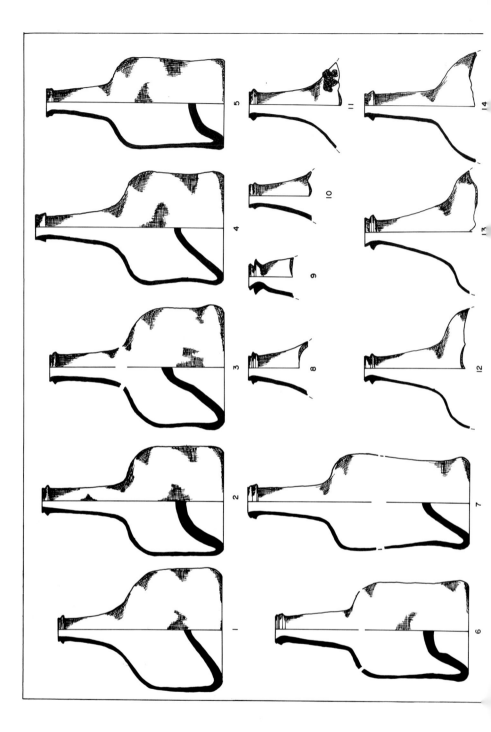

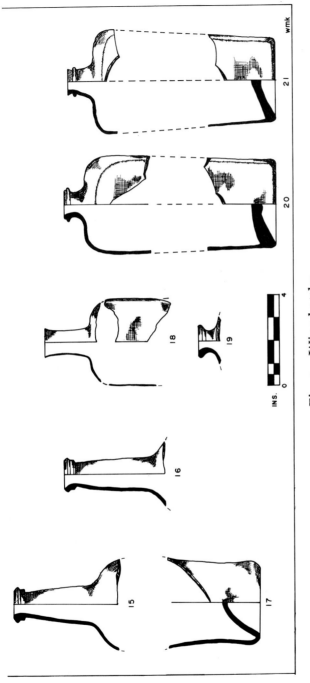

Fig. 50. Wine bottles.

Wineglasses, Tumblers, Pharmaceutical Bottles, and Other
Glass Items, Buckles, Candlestick and Drip Pan,
and Copper Teapot Spouts
Figure 51

1. Wineglass stem, lead glass, trumpet bowl, bulbous teardrop below bowl, conical foot, tapering stem, pontil mark on base, 1725–1760.[41] Pit C. (30E) W/112

2. Wineglass stem, lead glass, trumpet bowl, tapering stem without teardrop, 1735–1760.[42] Pit A. (7E³) W/113

3. Wineglass stem, lead glass, straight sides, probably bucket-shaped bowl type with a conical foot, base of bowl somewhat concave inside, 1730–1760.[43] (16C) W/114

4. Drinking glass or "rummer," lead glass, wheel engraved with a floral (sunflower?), arch, and pyramid design, probably had a thick bucket bowl, fragments could not be joined, engraving left rough and unpolished, 1760–1820.[44] Pit C. (30M) W/115

5. Tumbler base, lead glass, seven engraved "thumbprint" wheel engraved facets surround base, pontil scar ground flat, sloping sides, after ca. 1740.[45] (24B) W/116

6. Tumbler base, clear lead glass, sloping sides, slightly rounded at base, domed base with unground pontil scar, eighteenth century.[46] Pit C. (30E) W/117-A

7. Wineglass stem knop, lead glass, double row of beaded teardrops inside (fifteen in all) tiered pedestal at base with pontil scar, evidence of stem break at top, extremely thin connection between knop and stem, 1725–1750.[47] Surface. W/117-B

8. Pharmaceutical bottle neck and base fragments, pale blue-green glass, short tubular neck with everted and flattened rim, broad conical base, pontil scar, conjectural shape based on intact example, seventeenth and eighteenth centuries.[48] Pit B. (14B) W/118

9. Molded medicine phial, clear lead glass, lettering roughly molded in relief on side panel and side, probably reading BY THE KING'S ROYAL PATENT GRANTED TO ROBT TURLINGTON FOR HIS INVENTED BALSAM OF LIFE with LONDON on the side and JANUY 26, 1754 on the other, pontil scar on base, rectangular in section after 1754.[49] Pit C. (32C, 11A) W/119

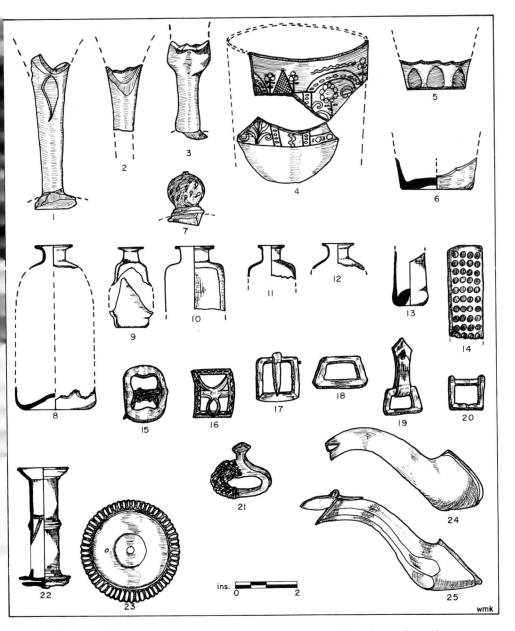

Fig. 51. Wineglasses, tumblers, pharmaceutical bottles, other glass items, buckles, candlestick and drip pan, and copper teapot spouts.

10. Molded pharmaceutical bottle neck, clear glass, everted and flattened rim, body square in section, paneled sides, extremely thin, late eighteenth–early nineteenth century. Pit C. (20C) W/120

11. Pharmaceutical bottle neck, pale blue-green glass, everted and flattened mouth, similar to no. 8 above, with narrower more sharply angled shoulders, eighteenth century. (30A) W/121

12. Pharmaceutical bottle neck, same glass color and features as no. 8 above but smaller in diameter. Pit B. (14B) W/122

13. Pharmaceutical bottle base, pale blue-green glass, heavy domed basal kick, rough pontil scar, 1760–1780.[50] Pit C. (30E) W/123

14. Brush head, bone, bristle holes taper toward base holes, reverse side grooved in line with bristle holes probably to serve as a guide for wire or gut bristles holding string. (2F) W/124

15. Shoe buckle, brass frame with iron tines, eighteenth century (?).[51] (3J) W/125

16. Shoe buckle, steel, rectangular frame decorated with series of scalloplike indentations along upper edges, eighteenth century.[52] Pit C. (30C) W/126

17. Harness buckle, iron, rectangular frame square sectioned, tang wrapped around frame, notched at lower corners, eighteenth century.[53] (31L) W/127

18. Harness buckle, iron, frame round in section on top side, other three sides flattened. Pit C. (30E) W/128

19. Harness buckle and leather fastener, iron, buckle similar to no. 18 above but smaller, fastener apparently riveted to leather strap. Pit C. (30E) W/129

20. Harness buckle (?), brass, cast and filed, tang bar round in section, other sides semicircular in section, filed notches near tang bar and center of opposite side. (15B) W/130

21. Harness strap swivel (?), iron, loop square in section. Pit C. (32C) W/131

22. Candlestick, made from single sheet of brass brazed together, column type banded in the middle and at the base, lever in stem moves lead piston which raised candle or aided in ejecting the burned stumps (see sectional view on left), weighted with brass disc at base for stability, remnants of thin drip pan and base section broken off, first half of the eighteenth century.[54] Pit C. (30H) W/132

23. Candlestick drip pan, brass, edged with elongated beading around rim, rivet hole in center, raised center, probably base to similar candlestick as no. 22 above, extremely thin, eighteenth century. (5L) W/133

24. Teakettle spout, sheet copper, end split, flattened where spout had been brazed to body, sheet brazed together along top, eighteenth century (?). (17A) W/134

25. Teakettle spout, sheet copper, under section of large end flattened into five facets, sheet brazed along top, hinged cover held with iron pin brazed to spout opening, flattened at large end where spout was brazed to body, eighteenth century. (8c) W/135

Cutlery, Spoons, Clay Tobacco Pipes, and Colono-Indian Pottery
Figure 52

1. Knife, iron with plate bone handle, handle decorated with a grooved chevron design, one bone plate missing, handle plates secured to haft with iron rivets, mid-eighteenth century.[55] (30B) W/136

2. Knife, iron with plate bone handle, plates secured with iron rivets, iron cap on handle terminal, mid-eighteenth century. Pit C. (30F) W/137

3. Knife, iron, faceted shoulders, flattened shank, mid-eighteenth century. (33B) W/138

4. Knife, iron, round heavy shoulders, flaring shank, first half of eighteenth century. (33B) W/139

5. Knife, iron, octagonal shoulder, broken round shank, dorsal ridge along top of blade, first half of eighteenth century.[56] (2H) W/140

6. Knife, iron, completely corroded, round shoulder and shank. (6E) W/141

7. Clasp knife, iron, handle plates missing but handle rivets in place, three piece construction riveted together, blade completely rusted away, curved handle, mid-eighteenth century.[57] (5B) W/142

8. Clasp knife, iron, similar curved handle to no. 7 above, apparently had small bone or wooden handle plates held in place by

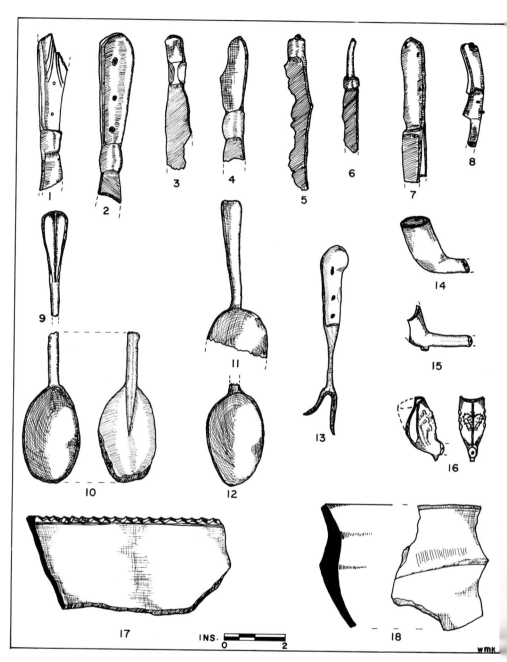

Fig. 52. Cutlery, spoons, clay tobacco pipes, and Colono-Indian pottery.

iron rivets, blade completely rusted away, eighteenth century.[58] (22B) W/143

9. Spoon handle, pewter, flaring terminal with central spinal ridge, mid-eighteenth century.[59] (2C) W/144

10. Spoon bowl, pewter, oval bowl, rat-tailed strengthening ridge on underside of base, handle semicircular in section, eighteenth century.[60] (7C) W/145

11. Spoon handle and bowl section, iron, handle junction with bowl is slightly off center, extremely corroded. (31L) W/146

12. Spoon bowl, latten, tinned to look like silver, worn only on one side as if used exclusively by right-handed person, three ribbed rat-tailed strengthening ridges on underside where bowl joins handle, first half of the eighteenth century.[61] (19D) W/147

13. Fork, iron with two plated bone handle, pistol-grip handle, handle held to shank by iron rivets, two tines, early eighteenth century.[62] (31A) W/148

14. Tobacco pipe bowl, clay, probably English, without heel or spur, bowl diameter 21 mm,* bowl depth 45 mm, $\frac{5}{64}''$ stem hole diameter, 1720–1780.[63] (19B) W/149

15. Tobacco pipe bowl and stem fragment, clay, probably English, flattened spur with deep mold mark on its base, $\frac{4}{64}''$ stem hole diameter, late eighteenth–early nineteenth century. (30B) W/150

16. Tobacco pipe bowl, clay, probably English, small broken spur, relief molded showing a crown on the middle of the upper side of bowl flanked by feathered ribbing, bowl depth 35 mm, stem hole diameter $\frac{6}{64}''$, late eighteenth–early nineteenth century. (9A) W/151

17. Large bowl rim fragment, Colono-Indian pottery, sand-tempered red-orange body fired black inside in places, notched rim, incised line below rim notches.[64] Pit C. (30E) W/152

18. Indian pot rim sherd, thickened and angled shoulder, everted rim, black body with orange in places on the surface, decorated with roughly parallel incised lines just above shoulder.[65] (5C) W/153

---

* Measurements of clay tobacco pipes will be given in millimeters on the exterior and 64ths of an inch for diameters of stemholes. This apparent lack of consistency results from using standard sized American drillbits to measure the stemholes as scholars in the field suggest.

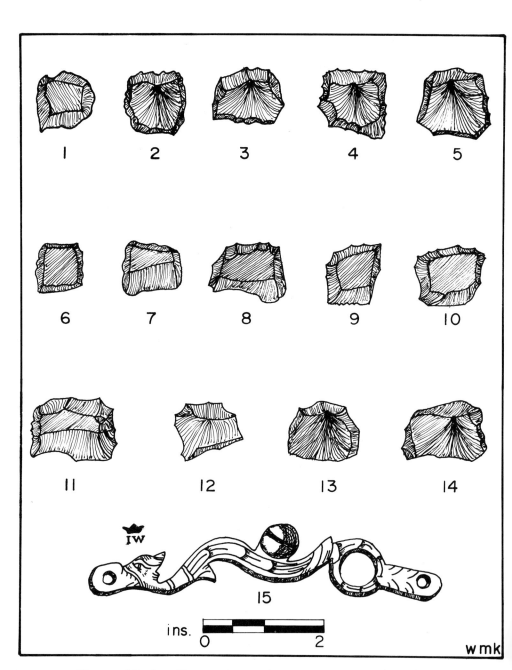

Fig. 53. Musket flints and spalls and a brass musket sideplate.

Musket Flints and Spalls and a Brass Musket Sideplate
Figure 53

1. Musket flint, English prismatic type, upper face concave.[66] (5G) W/154

2. Musket spall, grayish white chert, percussion point clearly discernible, roughly finished around the edges, the recovery of large chunks of this same stone bearing percussion marks and numerous worked chips of the same material suggest that this example and nos. 3–5 following may have been made on the site.[67] (27C) W/155

3. Musket spall, same as no. 2 above but slightly broader. (22B) W/156

4. Musket spall, same material and workmanship as nos. 1 and 2 above. (14B) W/157

5. Musket spall, same as nos. 2–4 above. (15B) W/158

6. Pistol flint, French, light honey-colored stone, prismatic type. (27C) W/159.

7. Musket flint, French, same stone as no. 6 above, prismatic type. (22B) W/160

8. Musket flint, same type and stone as nos. 6 and 7 above. Pit A. (7E) W/161

9. Musket flint, same type and stone as nos. 6–8 above, one side broken off. (16E) W/162

10. Musket flint, same type and stone as nos. 6–9 above. (2D) W/163

11. Large musket flint, same type and stone as nos. 6–10 above. (27C) W/164

12. Pistol or musket spall, same stone as nos. 6–11 above. (20A) W/165

13. Musket spall, same type and stone as no. 12 above. (15F) W/166

14. Musket spall, same type and stone as nos. 12 and 13 above. (2K) W/167

15. Musket ornamental side plate, cast brass with engraved dragon design iron hammer bolt head still attached, piece is roughly stamped on the reverse side of the dragon's head with what appears to be the initials *IW* surmounted by a crown (as shown); this piece was probably made by John Whatley, a London gunsmith working in the 1770s.[68] Pit E. (20B) Also fragment of same type of plate found in (1B) W/168

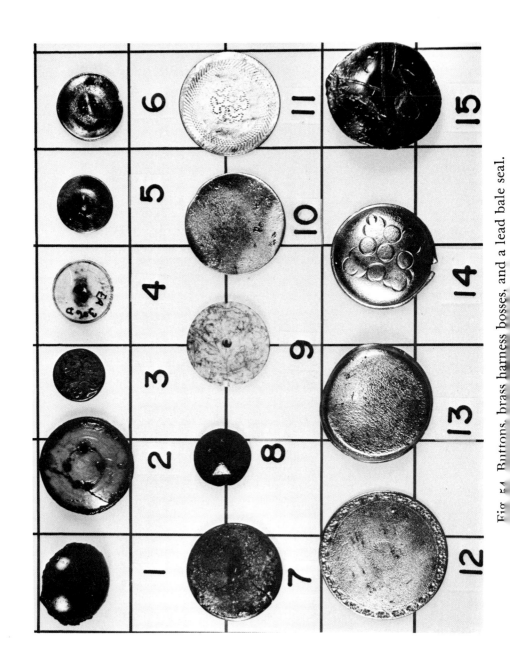

Fig. 54. Buttons, brass harness bosses, and a lead bale seal.

Buttons, Brass Harness Bosses, and a Lead Bale Seal
Figure 54

1. Button, brass-plated front, domed tin, iron back, brass wire eye, 21 mm in diameter, eighteenth century.[69] (15E) W/169

2. Button, flat tinned brass face crimped to a domed bone back, five holes appear through bone back (one apparently a mistake) which were made to take a crossed gut thread fastening loop, 25 mm diameter, eighteenth century.[70] (24C) W/170

3. Button, brass face with relief rococo floral design, face crimped to slightly domed bone back, brass wire eye, eighteenth century.[71] (1B) W/171

4. Button back, bone, same type as no. 3 above, slightly domed, brass wire eye, grooved along rim for crimping, 14 mm diameter, eighteenth century. (6D) W/172

5. Button, brass and tinned to look like silver, plain flat face, brass eye cast in place, spun back, 15 mm diameter, eighteenth–early nineteenth century. (31A) W/173

6. Button, brass and tinned to look like silver as no. 5 above, face slightly convex, eye cast in place, spun concave back, 17 mm diameter, eighteenth–early nineteenth century. Pit C. (30D) W/174

7. Button, brass and iron, thin sheet brass back crimped over iron core, face missing, brass wire eye, 25 mm diameter, eighteenth century (?). (6D) W/175

8. Button, cast and faceted black glass, brass eye pressed into back, 16 mm diameter, eighteenth century. (2C) W/176

9. Button, flat bone disk, 22 mm diameter, eighteenth–early nineteenth century. (1B) W/177

10. Button, flat brass disk, soldered loop eye missing, undecorated, 26 mm diameter, eighteenth–early nineteenth century. (16C) W/178

11. Button, flat brass disk tinned to look like silver as nos. 5 and 6 above, rouletted design stamped around front rim, brass wire eye soldered to back (broken off), dotted floral (?) design on the center, 26 mm diameter, eighteenth–early nineteenth century. (Unstratified) W/179

12. Button, flat brass disk with soldered brass eye (broken off), rouletted designs around rim and at center, 34 mm diameter, eighteenth–early nineteenth century. (3C) W/180

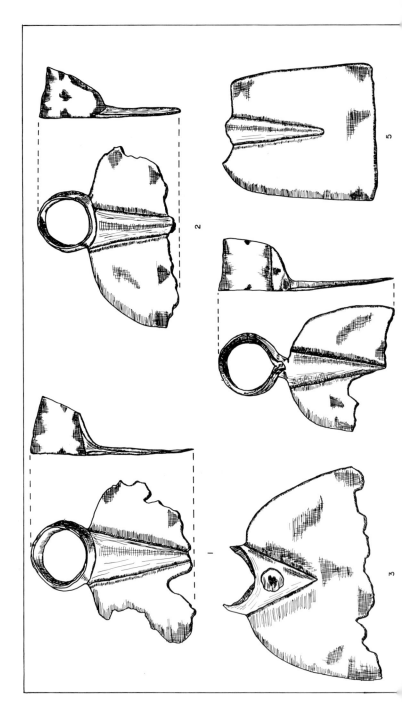

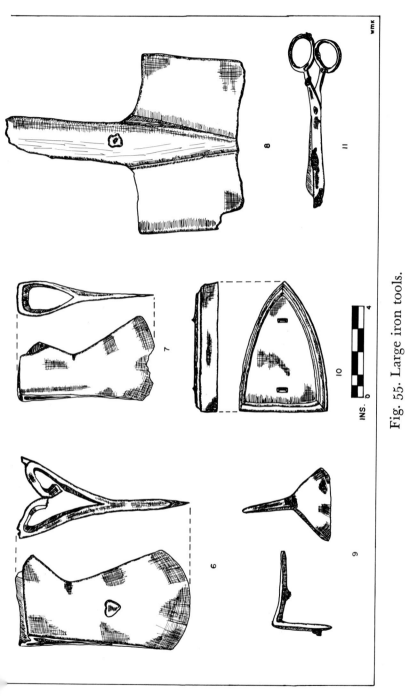

Fig. 55. Large iron tools.

13. Harness boss, stamped cast brass, probably anchored to the leather by an iron cotter pin or eye mounted within a small collar at center of back, 30 mm diameter, eighteenth century.[72] (30C) W/181

14. Harness boss, stamped cast brass, domed face engraved with five circles, grooved around rim, back concave with small brass collar as no. 13 above, probably securing iron eye of cotter pin fastener, 27 mm diameter. (4A) W/182.

15. Bale seal, lead, disk scratched with the number *51* (?) over a line over the number *65* (possibly the invoice number over the package number?), on the back there is some evidence that another disk (usually part of bale seals) has been broken off, two-eared fastener at the center of the back, eighteenth century.[73] Pit C. (30E) W/183

Large Iron Tools
Figure 55

1. Broad hoe, iron, unmarked, long narrow reinforcing spine, eighteenth century.[74] (20C) W/184

2. Broad hoe, iron, unmarked, long narrow reinforcing spine slightly off center. Pit C. (30M) W/185

3. Broad hoe, iron, possible circular maker's mark illegible, reinforcing spine broader and shorter than no. 1 and no. 2 above, eighteenth century. Pit C. (30K) W/186

4. Narrow hoe, iron, unmarked, rat-tailed reinforcing spine runs to socket and along base. Pit A. (7E) W/187

5. Narrow hoe blade, iron, unmarked, rat-tailed reinforcing spine similar to no. 4 above. Pit C. (30E) W/188

6. Large felling axe, iron, triangular eye, collapsed, bit beveled on both sides, marked on one side with heart-shaped symbol, weight 4 lbs.[75] Pit C. (30K) W/189

7. Felling axe or hatchet, iron, teardrop-shaped eye, triangular eye tabs, unmarked, weight 1 lb., often referred to as "Indian trade axe." Pit C. (30K) W/190

8. Spade, iron, shank made to wrap around wooden handle which was secured by nails driven through the front side, shaft ridge extends halfway down blade to serve as reinforcing spine, eighteenth century. Pit C. (30E) W/191

9. Small hand hoe, iron, grain marks from wooden handle still visible on shank. (21E) W/192

10. Flatiron, two iron handle weld marks (?) on upper face, weight 3 lbs.[76] Pit C. (30E) W/193

11. Scissors, iron, upper eye made for two fingers, lower eye for one, loops, eye and hafts square in section.[77] (8C) W/194

Hand Tools and Locks
Figure 56

1. Half-round file, iron, crosshatched grooves, possible maker's mark below handle (illegible). (7A) W/195

2. Half-round file, iron, grooves run in one direction only, possible maker's mark as no. 1 above (illegible), tapering handle. Pit C. (30E) W/196

3. Triangular file, iron, handle square in section and tapering, grooves completely rusted away. Pit C. (30J) W/197

4. Triangular file, iron, handle tapered and rectangular in section. Grooved in one direction only. (2A) W/198

5. Pincers or "nippers," iron, handles square in section, blade sharpened for cutting, handles stamped with the letter *I* or *L* near rivet.[78] (7B) W/199

6. Gimlet, iron, one end flattened to keep blade from twisting in handle, blade threaded at end and hollowed out above to allow bored wood to escape from hole, one of three such tools found on the site, the latter two are 3½ inches long. (8C, 17H, 18F) W/200

7. Drill bit, iron, completely rusted, probably produced a ⅜″ hole, handle end flattened as no. 6 above. (19A) W/201

8. Dividers, iron, movable leg broken off, bulb terminal, leg half round in section.[79] (27B) W/202

9. Saw blade fragment, iron. (16A) W/203

10. Object of unknown purpose (possibly brick mason's joint scoring tool?), iron, apparently had been flattened and clinched over end of wooden handle, blade neither sharpened nor pointed, commonly found on eighteenth-century sites.[80] (7D) W/204

11. Door lock bolt, iron, probably from plate stock lock, similar to no. 16 below, eighteenth–early nineteenth century.[81] (22D) W/205

12. Key, iron, shank round in section and hollow at tip. (31L) W/206

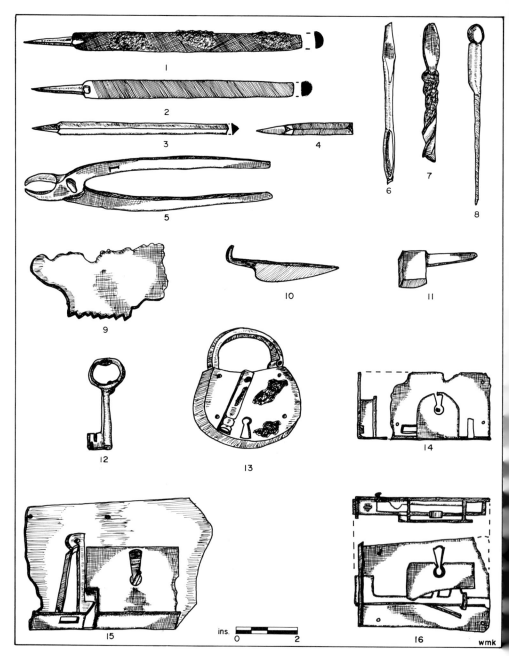

Fig. 56. Hand tools and locks.

13. Padlock, iron, typical bag-shaped body, brass and iron were used to make the keyhole cover which pivoted at the top, latch slightly rectangular in section, body 20 mm thick, almost completely corroded, eighteenth century.[82] Pit C. (30M) W/207

14. Chest, desk or trunk lock (?), iron, half-round ward, post in center of keyhole to take hollow-shanked key, simple rectangular sliding bolt, holes for fasteners at the corners of plate (side view drawing shown on right) Pit E. (20C) W/208

15. Door rim lock, iron, post and hollow key type as above (key shown above, no. 12, may well have fit this lock as blade is the right width); apparently the bolt was mounted on the door jamb. From there it slid into the lock mechanism whereby the pointed latch would then secure it in place. It therefore could be released only by turning the key. Tapering iron back plate, rectangular ward. (31G) W/209

16. Plate stock lock, iron, similar to no. 11 above, tapering backplate, eighteenth–early nineteenth century.[83] Pit C. (30D) W/210

Saddle Parts, Bridle Bits and Cowbells
Figure 57

1. Saddle cantle plate, iron, V-shaped rising in the center to fit the contour of the horse, extremely corroded, five nail holes (four with nails still in place). (Note: the large dotted lines are shown only to illustrate the positioning of this piece and the other parts of the saddle described below. The drawing is not based on any saddle of the period.) Seventeenth and eighteenth centuries.[84] Pit C. (30L) W/211

2. "Horn" saddle pommel, iron, completely rusted but the shape is basically retained, knob bent at approximately a 30° angle from neck and body, rivet with ½" head driven through back section, large nail (?) projecting through underside just below neck and body junction, body appears somewhat ridged down the middle, drawn in position above top view of front plate (discussed below), seventeenth and eighteenth centuries.[85] Pit C. (30M) W/212

3. Saddletree frontplate and underplate, iron, front view of same item shown in place under pommel (no. 2) above, two

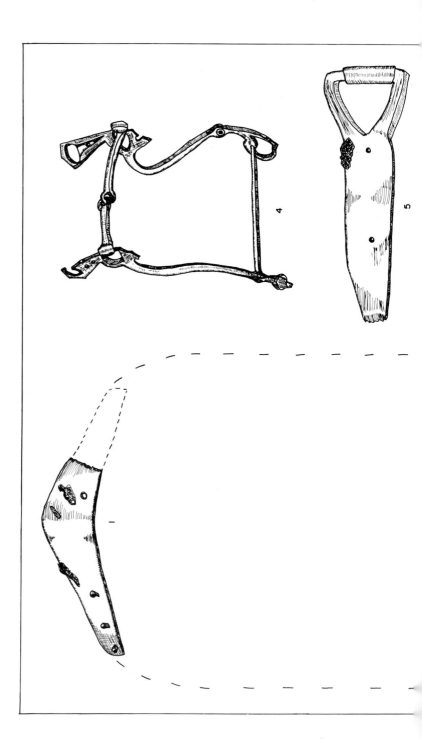

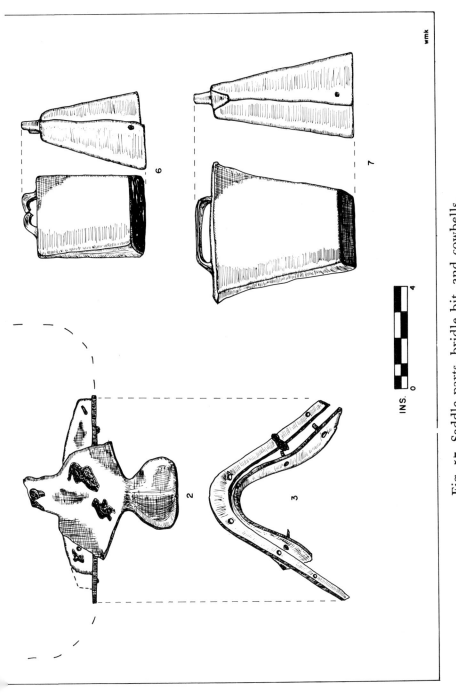

INS.

Fig. 57. Saddle parts, bridle bit, and cowbells.

pieces found in position as shown, extremely corroded, front plate pierced by six nail holes, five nails still in position, one end broken off, underplate pierced by five nail holes (three nails remain in place). When viewed from the top (no. 2 above) the front edge is straight whereas the back edge tapers in toward the front. The presence of the nails in all pieces suggests that the saddle body was made of wood then covered with leather. Seventeenth and eighteenth centuries.[86] Pit C. (30H) W/213, W/214

4. Curb bridle bit, iron, typical S-shaped cheek pieces, jointed bit, bar separator near lower loops served to keep cheek pieces apart, both cheek pieces have been brazed (?) together just below small hole in lower section of the arms (repair?), late seventeenth and eighteenth centuries.[87] Pit C. (30E) W/215

5. Object of uncertain purpose, iron, stirrup-shaped eye at one end made to take a strap as evidenced by the thin roller wrapped around it, bar square in section at base, lower section of piece flattened and pierced by two nail holes, broken off at end opposite the eye, possibly this piece had been nailed to a wagon or carriage to secure the harness. Pit C. (30J) W/216

6. Cowbell, sheet brass and iron alloy, extremely corroded, square shoulders, straight bodied but triangular as viewed from the side, rectangular collar loop at top, clapper bar at top of the interior runs parallel to the short sides, made from a single sheet of metal riveted down one side.[88] Pit C. (30K) W/217

7. Cowbell, sheet brass and iron alloy, extremely corroded, flat top with sharply angled shoulders and tapering sides, base considerably narrower than shoulders, triangular body when viewed from the side, shoulders formed by triangular fold in metal as shown, made from single sheet of metal folded and then riveted down on both sides, rectangular collar loop at top, clapper bar at top of the interior also runs parallel to the sides as no. 6 above.[89] Pit C. (30E) W/218

Hinges, Pintles, Hooks, Bolts, Nails, and Other Metal Items
Figure 58

1. T-shaped door hinge, iron, crosspiece pierced with three nail holes, possibly marked with L-shaped maker's mark. (9A) W/219

2. Strap from T-shaped door hinge, iron, part of terminal loop broken off, pierced by three nail holes. Pit C. (30E) W/220

3. End of strap hinge, iron, pierced by two nail holes, probably ended in flattened flare as no. 4 below. (2D) W/221

4. End of strap hinge, iron, evidence of nail holes through flared end and at break in opposite end. (33B) W/222

5. Strap hinge (?), iron, strap pierced with a nail or rivet hole at break, end flared and had been riveted to section of metal of about the same thickness. Pit E. (20C) W/223

6. Strap hinge, iron, broken off at the end, pierced with two nail holes, possibly stamped with a heart-shaped mark between the two holes, interior diameter of loop 9 mm.[90] (15B) W/224

7. Small strap hinge, iron, extremely corroded, no evidence of nail holes, loop interior diameter probably 6 mm. (32C) W/225

8. Butterfly hinge piece (?), iron, possibly from a trunk, extremely corroded, pierced by four nail holes, pin 5 mm in diameter. Pit C. (30E) W/226

9. Cross piece from T-shaped door hinge (?), iron, pierced by four countersunk holes (screw holes?), pin hole diameter 7 mm. (16C) W/227

10. Crosspiece from T-shaped hinge (?), iron, pierced by two countersunk holes, loop section broken off, smaller than similar section of piece illustrated in no. 1 above. (20A) W/228

11. Large door hinge pintle, iron, pivot bar 12 mm in diameter, spike arm rectangular in section tapering to point, flattened at the elbow from being driven into door frame. (20B) W/229

12. Small hinge pintle, iron, pin 4 mm in diameter, spike arm rectangular in section 4 mm thick with pointed end broken off. (21D) W/230

13. Large door hinge pintle, iron, pivot bar round in section and pointed, spike arm rectangular in section and pointed as no. 11 above, elbow worked flat. Pit C. (30C) W/231

14. Small hinge pintle, iron, pivot arm 7 mm in diameter, spike arm rectangular in section tapering to a point. Pit C. (30C) W/232

15. Pin, iron, possibly from large door strap hinge, greatest diameter 10 mm, round in section, bulbous head. (18E) W/233

16. Latch (?), iron, shaft round in section flattened at both hook and swivel ends, swivel pin 3 mm in diameter. (9B) W/234

17. Latch (?), iron, 3 mm thick, metal separated on one end. (31L) W/235

18. Latch end (?), cast brass, swivel end only, hole 7 mm in

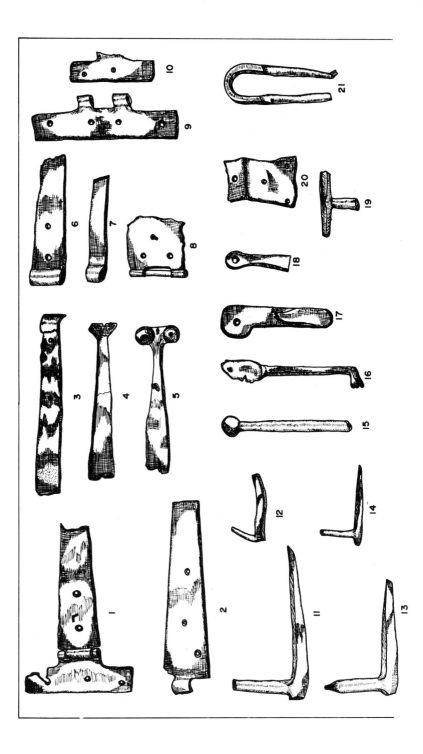

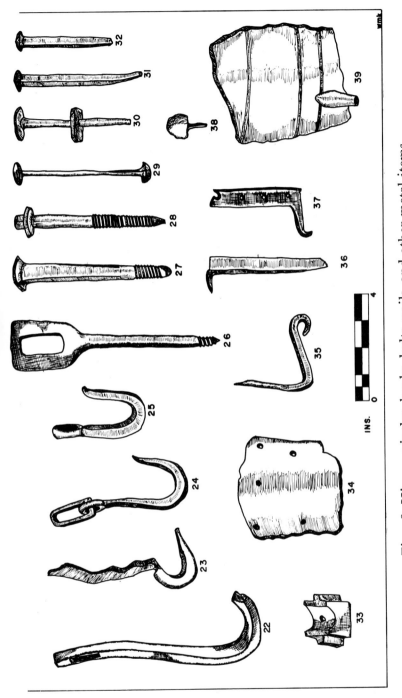

Fig. 58. Hinges, pintles, hooks, bolts, nails, and other metal items.

diameter, arm goes from 1 mm to 2 mm thick from loop to broken end, polished on one side, rough cast finish on opposite side. (28A) W/236

19. Object of unknown purpose, iron, perhaps a shutter latch (?), crosspiece rectangular in section, shaft round in section. Pit C. (30E) W/237

20. Strap, iron, pierced by four nail holes, apparently had been bent at right angle near broken end, possibly used as a reinforcing piece from the corner of a trunk (?). Pit E. (20G) W/238

21. Large staple, iron, loop rectangular in section 6 mm × 10 mm, spiked ends flattened and tapered. Pit C. (30E) W/239

22. Large hook, iron, shaft square in section 13 mm thick, long rectangular hole near terminal measuring 5 mm × 30 mm, probably made to take a securing wedge or key, hook end broken off and roughly rounded. Pit C. (30E) W/240

23. Hook, iron, stamped with what appears to be the number 5 on the flattened strap above the hook, the thinness of this strap suggests that the hook had projected from a brick wall with the strap bonded into the mortar joint (?), hook section rectangular in section. Pit C. (32C) W/241

24. Chain hook, iron, two chain links connected to eye chain links, too corroded to estimate size of links, only the core of the hook was left after cleaning (therefore diameter shown is considerably smaller than the original).[91] (18E) W/242

25. Hook, iron, loop at terminal 20 mm in interior diameter, scrolled at the hook end, generally rectangular in section. Pit C. (30G) W/243

26. Object of unknown purpose, iron, shaft threaded at the tip but rectangular in section above, terminal flattened into a rectangular eye somewhat broader at the top than at the base, interior edge of eye slightly worn on the right and lower edges (as shown). (1B in front of doorway, outside the house). W/244

27. Large spike, iron, vaguely threaded at the tip and rounded about a third of the way up the shaft, square in section above, square flat head, blunted end. (22B) W/245

28. Bolt, iron, washer welded to shaft ⅜″ below top, shaft above washer is square in section presumably to take a ⅜″ wrench, shaft below washer is round in section, thread length 2¾″, shaft diameter approximately ⁷⁄₁₆″.[92] Pit E. (20C) W/246

29. Large rivet, iron, domed heads ⅞″ diameter, shaft round in

section, possibly from a boat or carriage, one of two identical rivets found at the site. (31L and 9D) W/247

30. Bolt and nut, iron, extremely corroded, domed head, threads completely rusted away, nut measures approximately 1⅛″ × 1⅛″ × 3⁄16″. Pit C. (30J) W/248

31. Spike, iron, rose-pointed head, rectangular in section, 5⁄16″ × ¼″. (5A) W/249

32. Spike, iron, rose-pointed head, rectangular in section, ⅜″ × ¼″. (7A) W/250

33. Object of unknown purpose, iron, possibly a wagon wheel wedge key, larger at base than at the top (as shown) suggesting its use as a wedge key, hole through center for lubrication (?). (31H) W/251

34. Plate, iron, pierced by nail holes as shown, rounded corners, markedly convex (as shown), broader at the top than at the bottom.[93] Pit C. (30E) W/252

35. Hook, iron, looped arm rectangular in section, opposite arm round and pointed and apparently made to be driven into wood, possibly made to support wire lantern hanger (?).[94] Pit C. (30D) W/253

36. Wedge-shaped masonry spike (?), iron, shaft rectangular in section, head flat, cleat on head apparently clinched wood to masonry.[95] (7C) W/254

37. Object of uncertain purpose, possibly the adjustment arm from a chimney crane, iron, scrolled terminal, pierced by four holes (adjustments), one end broken off.[96] Pit C. (30D) W/255

38. Object of unknown purpose, iron, possibly a chair foot cleat, bulbous head on what appears to be a nail shaft. (12C) W/256

39. Cauldron, iron, body and handle fragment, decorated with encircling ridges, round tapering handle post, wall diameter 4 mm.[97] Pit C. (30D) W/257

Appendix A

STRATIFICATION OF ILLUSTRATED ARTIFACTS

ER Number   Description

Pit A: Trash Pits

$7E^2$-E^3 Yellow sandy fill with bits of oyster shell, interior loophole platform

$7E^4$, E^5, 17E, H, J   Dark brown sandy loam with flecks of wood ash

$17E^2$ Concentrated wood ash

$7K$, L, M, $17E^2$-E^5 Light brown sandy loam with flecks of wood ash

Pit B

14B   1. Grayish sandy loam with bits of oyster shell, concentration of wine bottle glass, interior loophole platform

2. Grayish sandy loam with bits of oyster shell immediately below concentration of wine bottle glass, interior loophole platform

Pit C: Well

30C, D, F   1. Black sandy fill with oyster shell

30G, H   2. Light brown sandy fill with oyster shell, well fill

30J   3. Light gray sandy fill with brick dust and oyster shell, well fill

30K, L   4. Light gray sandy fill with wood ash, well fill

32C, 30E, M   5. Light gray sandy fill with oyster shell, well washout and fill

ER Number	Description
30N	6. Mottled yellow sandy wash, with bricks from well washout
30P	7. Miscellaneous debris at bottom of well

Pit D

12B	1. Dark loam with concentration of brickbats, interior loophole platform foundation
12C	2. Dark gray loam with wood ash and bits of oyster shell, interior loophole platform foundation
12D, E	3. Concentration of shell along west wall, interior loophole platform foundation

Pit E

20B	1. Black sandy loam and oyster shell
20C	2. Light gray sandy fill
—	3. Decomposed tabby
20G	4. Yellow sandy fill
—	5. Decomposed tabby (?)
—	6. Yellow sandy fill

Deposits Predating the Tabby Period, ca. 1737–1740

4F	Yellow sandy loam with flecks of gray ash and bits of oyster shell
6F	Dark sandy loam, postmold (?)
6J	Dark brown sandy loam (old topsoil?)
16F	Mottled yellow sandy loam beneath bottom of tabby wall
21E	Mottled yellow sand with bits of oyster shell below base of tabby house wall
19D	Hard packed mottled yellow sandy loam with bits of oyster shell below base of tabby house wall
31N	Light yellow sand with ash, shallow pit NW section of square
30P	White sandy fill around well, builder's trench

Deposits Associated with Tabby Construction, ca. 1739–1744

2H	Concentration of oyster shell and lime between south wall of house and south tabby floor block

ER Number	Description
2J	Yellow sandy fill beneath tabby floor block (removed)
5G	Light gray sand, with flecks of wood ash and bits of oyster shell abutting east wall of tabby house
5L	Concentration of oyster shell and lime along south wall (builder's debris?)
6H	Yellow sandy fill (below tabby floor?)
6K	Concentration of oyster shell and lime along south wall (builder's trench?)
7J	Light gray sand with flecks of wood ash even with base of loophole platform and main wall, SW bastion
8C	Light gray sand with flecks of wood ash in front of middle west doorway of house
8J	Fill under tabby building wall immediately adjacent to chimney foundation
9D	Light gray sand with flecks of wood ash and bits of oyster shell (post brick pier)
12E	Concentration of oyster shell and lime along west wall of loophole platform foundation
16E	Light gray sand and lime spread even with base of tabby wall
17G	Light gray sand concentrated with oyster shell along exterior west wall and associated with its base
20J	Concentration of oyster shell along east wall interior
31H	Light gray sand with concentrated oyster shell along exterior of west wall

Other Deposits Containing Illustrated Artifacts

1B	Black sandy loam with oyster shell immediately below topsoil, 1783–?
2C	Oyster shell spread along tabby floor blocks immediately below topsoil, 1800–1820
2D	Brick rubble and shell spread in slot in wall immediately in front of brickbat foundation next to chimney foundation, 1800–1820
3C	Scattered brick and shell immediately below topsoil, destruction level of building (?), first quarter of nineteenth century

ER Number	Description
3D	Fill in "modern trench," unstratified
3J	Disturbed repair (?) pit inside tabby and brickbat oven, 1750–?
5B	Dark loam with oyster shell immediately below topsoil, not datable artifacts
5C	Test trench in "modern trench" area, unstratified
5E	Fill in "modern trench," unstratified
6D	Pocket of oyster shell next to building wall section immediately below topsoil, first quarter of nineteenth century
6E	Fill in "modern trench," unstratified
7B	Posthole adjacent to southeast corner to tabby loophole platform foundation immediately below topsoil, eighteenth century
7C	Fill in "modern trench," immediately below topsoil, unstratified
9B	Shell and dark loam spread immediately below topsoil, first half of eighteenth century
15B	Mottled brown and yellow sand with oyster shell immediately below topsoil, 1790–1810
15F	Small depression (root hole?) filled with oyster shell, gray sandy loam immediately below 15B, northwest corner of trench, first half of eighteenth century
16C	Dark loam with shell immediately below topsoil, 1785–?
17C	Gray loam with shell immediately below topsoil, first half of eighteenth century
18B	Dark loam with shell, plaster, and window glass immediately below topsoil, 1800–
18D	Top of yellow sandy fill (had been below removed tabby floor) immediately below topsoil, first half of eighteenth century
18E	Light gray fill with powdered oyster shell immediately below topsoil west of tabby partition wall (decomposed tabby floor level?), 1754–?
19B	Scattered brickbat and shell spread immediately below

ER Number	Description
	topsoil (building destruction level?), eighteenth century
21D	Gray and black wood ash in front of northwest building doorway immediately below hard-packed yellow clay level (21B), first half of eighteenth century
22B	Dark loam and shell immediately below topsoil, 1740
22D	Dark loam, shell, and brickbats, northwest half of trench (disturbed?), 1740–?
24B	Dark loam and shell immediately below topsoil building exterior, late eighteenth century
24C	Yellow sand and shell immediately below 24B, no datable artifacts
25B	Mottled yellow sand and shell immediately below topsoil, no datable artifacts
27B	Dark loam with shell immediately below topsoil, mid-eighteenth century
27C	Oyster shell spread immediately below 27B, southwest corner of trench, first half of eighteenth century
31B	Fill in "modern trench" wall interior, unstratified
31G	Bottom of "topsoil" wall exterior
31J	Circular disturbance (robbed well?), north end of trench, unstratified
31L	Sandy brown loam with shell immediately below 31G (see above), 1720–?
33B	Light gray loam with shell immediately below topsoil, first half of eighteenth century

 *Appendix B*

A LIST OF PURCHASES OF NOBLE JONES AT THOMAS RASBERRY'S STORE IN SAVANNAH, GEORGIA
1759–1760 *

1759 Dr. Colonel Noble Jones to Thomas Rasberry Dr . .

	31	To Ballance due to me this Day . . .	–15(?)–
	10	2 shoe brushes	0– 1– 0
	7	2 yds. shallon	0– 4–10
		" " Donvlas Thread	0– 3– 0
	18	8 yds. Edenburts at 10	0– 6– 0
		2 pr. womans stockings, Padlock	0–11–10
	21	1 sett pinchbeck Buckells	0– 2–12
	26	¾ yd. Shallon	0– 1– 4
Mar.	5	2 yds. Narrow Blue Cloth	0 ?
	17	1 qu. Rum 2⁴ gunpowder	0– 9– 9
	28	¾ Donvlas 2 yds. ribbon	0– 1– 0
Apr.	9	4 Pr. Hinges at 10 1 pr. ditto	0– 6– 0
	14	1 gall. rum 5/9 1 pr. Hinges	0– 7– 1
	19	1 Pr. Large HL Hinges	0– 3– 2
	21	10 Pit Saw Files	0– 5–10
	"	4 While Rope, 1 Horse Bell	0– 6– 2
	21	1 broad axe	0– 5– 9
May	1	1 pr. Hinges 8th 2/Stock Lock	0– 2– 6
	3	1 Hair Broom 1/8 1 dust Brush	0– 2– 2
		1 Copper Tea Kettle	0–16– 6
		6 white stone plates 4/. . 2 stone dishes	0– 9– 0
		1 Doz. Knives & Forks	0– 7– 0

---

* "Noble Jones, Noble Wimberly Jones, George Jones Letter Book," University of Georgia Libraries, Athens, Ga.

	27	1 Closet Lock 1/2. . 1 doz wood screws	0– 1–10
	28	Geo Shop. . 1 bushel salt	0– 4– 0
		2 gns. Rum 1 Hasp & Staples	0–11– 9
	29	1 Hat. .1/2. .¼ Thread Pipes 3	0– 2– 5
		28 yd. Edenburgs	1– 2–11
		3½ yds. check 1 rule	0– 4–10
		2½ yds. Gardix 1 Handkerchief	0– 6– ¾
June	14	1 Tea 19 Funnel	0– 7– 3
	8	2 Deer Skins 100 8ᵈ Nails	0– 7–1(?)
	20	1 Pr. Hinges	0–1(?)–4
July	9	20 yds. netted gauze	1–10– 0
	12	1 pˢ manchester Binding	0– 1– 7
	15	1 Padlock 8ᵈ 2 powder	0– 4– 4
Aug.	10	2 gunpowder	0– 3– 8
		To Premium of Insurance on a Cash Indigo sent to London	2– 6–11¾
		Interest paid on said premium	0– 1– 9

1760 Dr. Bros over(?)
omitted 26th April last

		2 p HL Hinges	0– 4– 3
		1 p dovetail dᵉ	0– 0– 3
		200 8ᵈ Nails 200 10ᵈ nails do 1/6	0– 2– 8
		1 Pr. Sheeting 74 yds a 1/9	6– 9– 6
		1 flanders Bed Tick	1–10– 0
		2 China Bowls 7/6 & 1/4	0– 8–10
		1 Pr. Dovlas 38/ 1 bottle snuff 3/6	2– 1– 6
Oct.	14	12 Sugar 6/ the 24th 1½ Spikes	0– 6– 9
	29	2½ larel Rope	0– 1– 3
Nov.		2 p. Hinges at 8	0– 1– 4
	3	1 Sugar dish 10º 1 Stock Lock	0– 2– 8
Dec.	4	3, 7 white Rope a 8ᵉ	0– 2– 3½
	15	1 box Wafers 1 Horse Bell 2/6	0– 3– 6

1760 To the Estate of Tho Rasberry Dr.(?)

Dec.	3	To Balance due this day brought forward	40–13– 0

1760

Jan.	5	2 gallons okum 5/9	0–11– 6

	10	½ yd. muslin	0– 7– 6
	16	10 sugar 07	0–10– 6
	28	1 falling axe 4/3 300 10ᵈ nails	0– 6– 6
Feb.	18	500 10 Nails 3/6 1 Iron Pott	0– 5– 6
Mar.	10	1¼ yd. binding	0– 0– 2¼
Apr.	16	13½ Sugar	0– 6– 9
May	26	2 broad Hoes, 5/1 falling axe 4/3	0– 9– 3
		3 Thread	0– 6– 6
	27	1 quart brown bowl	0– 0–10
June	22	2 black Tea Pots 10ᵈ 5ᵈ	0– 7– 3
Aug.	3	2 gunpowder	0– 3– 4
Sept.	12	12 small shot 4 1 Lump Lime	0– 4– 7
Sep.	18	12 Broad Axes	1–10– 0
		6 Sickles 100 20ᵈ Nails	0– 5– 3
		and on exchanging a Lime	0– 0– 3

Dur the 2 nd Octo. 1762(?)   54/2/10¼

Appendix C

NOBLE WIMBERLY JONES'S INVENTORY
(1807) *

Inventory & Appraisement of personal Property belonging to the Estate of Doctor Noble Wimberly Jones, late of Savannah, deceased.

Negroes

Walley	10
Binah	200
August (very old)	1
Old Venus his wife	1
Old Sarah	1
Old Ben	50
Venus his wife	200
Stephen ⎫	400
little Ben ⎪	300
Tom ⎬ their children	150
Harvey ⎪	100
Clarinda ⎭	275
Sam	450
Juliet and her infant Tyra	450
Leah	200
Frank	150
Memba & her infant Sue	450
Phabe ⎫	200
Margaret ⎬ Her children	150
Adam ⎭	275

* Inventory of Noble Wimberly Jones, Chatham County Archives, Savannah, Ga.

Tyia	400
Jenny	150
Harry	125
Philander	100
Nelly	200
Betty & her infant Charles	450
Nancy	200
Adam	125
Binah	100
Sue & Jack her infant	450
Morris	200
Claripa	200
Molly	200
Carries over	6,913
Amount brought over	6,913
Abraham	100
Molly	400
Bob	100
Tenah	100
Charlotte & George her child	450
Hampshire	
&	1
Pendar	
May	450
Jenny (his wife)	300
John	225
Sarah his wife & mother of Betty	300
Prince	450
Simon	300
Joe (deaf)	100
Milly	225
Comba	1
Lambeth	300
Jim	375
March	450
Surry	450

Old Tenah		50
Grace		100
Di		200
Elijah		450
Rachel		1
		12,791
	Brought forward	12,791

Stock at Plantation

3 Bulls		
6 Oxen & Steers	36 Head at $5	180
27 Cows & Calves		
20 old Sheep		
7 lambs	.at $2	54
Old Cart & 5 old Cart Wheels		2
" Waggon		20
Lot of Old Iron		5
7 Crop cut & whip Saws		7
5 Hoggs		20
1 Wind fan		5
1 Double set drawers		30
1 Old desk		2
25 Windsor Chairs at $1		25
19 Fancy d° 2		38
10 Mahogany d° . . . . 50 ch		8
1 Bedchair		5
4 Wash stands		8
1 Mahogany Cooler		5
1 Square Mahogany box & contents		4
2 . . . .d° Breakfast table at $4		8
1 Small d° Dining table		5
2 Round d° tea tables . . . .at $2		4
2 Mahogany knife cases & knives at $20		40
1 lot of Glass		40
1 pr. old small carriage wheels & iron axel tree		2
1 lot of table china		25
1 lot of Crockery		30

1 D° Tea-China	10
1 Sideboard	20
1 bookcase & drawers	20
1 old Sofa	15
1 set mahogany Dining Tables	30
1 Candle stand	3
2 old Safes, 1 pine bed stead & Desk	4
1 mirror	5
Carried forward	13,472

Amount brought forward	13,472
1 best set of double drawers	40
1 book case with desk & drawers	25
1 oto bureau	5
1 small Thermometer	8
2 pr. steelbow spectacles	2
1 mahogany liquor case & bottles	15
2 walking canes	3
2 umbrellas	5
2 Rose blankets	6
11 Quilts & Coverlets	20
2 Gauze pavillions	4
9 large table Cloths	30
1 lot of bed & window curtains	30
1 pr. of Russia sheets & 3 pillow cases	5
2 ozinburgh Sheets, 1 d° table Cloth, 1 Bag & 3 d° towells	3
5 mattrapes . . . . . .at $5	25
4 featherbeds at $20	80
9 pillows 2 $1	9
4 bolsters 0 $2	8
Wearing apparel	2
3 glass Candle Shades & 5 D° Candlesticks	15
1 old musket	1
1 Screen	3
1 common bedstead high posts	2
1 old Cot	1

12 brass Candlesticks 2 D° metal, 1 d° Tin	6	
2 pewter Cranes	5	
3 lamps		75
5 pair of Snuffers & 2 snuffer stands	2	
2 Coffee mills	1	
1 plate warmer & 1 footman	5	
3 Tea Kettles	2	
1 pr. brass Seales	1	
Medicines & Shop furniture	25	
Pewter plates, basons & dishes	6	
1 Chaffing dish & 3 Trevots	1	
Tin ware & Tin Shower bath	25	
Juggs & Jars (the whole)	6	
	13,904	75

Amount brought forward	13,904	75
Knives & forks, Iron spoons, oyster knives etc	5	
Tool chest & tools	5	
2 Stills	3	
1 Hearth Rug	5	
3 Carpets	20	
1 lot of Waiters, break baskets & bottle (?)	10	
2 pair of plated candlesticks	10	
1 lot of bells	1	
4 fenders, 2 pr. brass andirons, 3 iron d°		
4 shovells (?)	30	
1 large iron pot	8	
1 Copper kettle	10	
1 large d°	8	
1 Iron kettle	3	
4 Clothes brushes	1	
2 pr. of Quern stones . . . . . .at $8	16	
2 old bed steads	10	
1 iron Chest	15	
1 lot of bottles	2	
2 demijohns	3	
9 Chests & Cases	9	

10	Trunks at $2	20
1	Gold watch, steel chain, & gold Seal & key	75
1	pair of pocket pistols	12
2	three quire blank books & 4 quires of writ. Paper	2
1	Tea Urn	5
	Kitchen Furniture	18
3	Chimney Grates . . . . . .at $10	30
2	dressing Glasses	5
3	iron chimney backs	3
1	pair of gold mounted spectacles & silver case	20
1	d° silver d° green case	4

1	Silver Tankard			
1	" teapot			
1	small d°			
1	silver Coffeepot & stand			
1	" half pint mug			
2	" milk pots	ounces		
2	" butter boats			
1	" large Spoon	165¼ at $1.00	165	25
16	" table Spoons . . . .6 teaspoons			
1	" nutmeg case & grater			
2	" Sugar Tongs			

Carried over	14,438
Amount brought over	14,438

1	mahogany Medicine chest	6
10	vols. Books at $1	10
	Pamphlets	2
1	Chair & harness	30

Dollars —	14,486

Appendix D

INVENTORY OF ARTIFACTS RECOVERED FROM BRICK WELL AT WORMSLOW

Pit C: Well Inventory

Ceramics (129 Vessels)

Slipware:

    4 dotted yellow posset pots
    5 trailed yellow posset pots
    1 mottled brown on yellow cup (?)
    6 notched rim brown trailed dishes
    1 dark brown trailed yellow bowl
    1 dark brown trailed yellow dish
    1 dark brown yellow branch pattern dish
    1 dark brown trailed yellow dish
    1 rust yellow banded bowl
    1 rust trailed and dotted yellow vessel
    1 rust wavy trailed yellow bowl
    1 black brown trailed yellow bowl
    1 orange trailed green vessel
    1 marbled tan and brown vessel banded in yellow
  —
  26

Delftware:

    1 blue on light blue floral cup
    1 blue on light blue floral mug (?)
    1 white ointment pot
    1 light blue vessel
    1 blue on white floral and banded cup
    1 blue overglaze red on light blue bowl
    1 large light blue punch bowl
  —
  7

Chinese Porcelain:
> 1 bowl
> 7 blue banded cups
> 1 blue underglaze, red overglazed gilted vessel
> 1 blue on light blue bowl
> 1 saucer
> ___
> 11

White Saltglazed Stoneware:
> 6 plain white cups
> 5 plain white saucers
> 3 scratch blue saucers
> 1 scratch blue cup
> 4 dot, diaper, and basket pattern molded plates
> 1 plain bonded plate or bowl
> 1 plain plate rim
> 1 scratch blue chamber pot
> ___
> 22

Gray Stoneware:
> 1 cobalt blue decorated banded vessel
> 1 gray storage jar
> ___
> 2

Brown Stoneware:
> 1 Bellarmine bottle (?)
> 2 large mottled brown jugs
> ___
> 3

Red Stoneware:
> 1 black glazed jug
> 1 brown glazed teapot
> 1 dry body teapot
> ___
> 3

Whieldon-Wedgwood Ware:
> 1 emerald green barley pattern molded plate
> 1 emerald green barley pattern molded bowl
> 1 emerald green cup
> 1 clouded ware tortoiseshell bead and reel pattern plate
> ___
> 4

Creamware:

    2 beaded rim cups
    1 bead and reel pattern saucer
    4 cups
    1 Royal pattern plate
    1 marbled orange and brown pepper (?)
    1 banded vessel
    ——
    10

Pearlware:

    2 blue shell-edged plates
    1 banded (?) yellow and brown hand-painted mug
    1 bowl banded in green
    1 plate hand-painted in blue
    1 clouded blue vessel
    ——
    6

Coarse Earthenware:

    1 small green pot
    1 green and red mug
    1 green mug
    1 salmon pitcher
    1 small caramel brown bowl
    2 mottled brown bowls
    1 yellow perforated bowl
    1 unglazed storage jar
    1 orange glazed storage jar
    1 honey brown glazed storage jar
    1 mottled salmon glazed storage jar
    1 maroon glazed storage jar
    1 mottled maroon glazed storage jar
    1 mottled green glazed storage jar
    1 dull yellow glazed storage jar
    1 orange red glazed storage jar
    1 caramel brown glazed creampan
    1 dark caramel brown glazed creampan
    1 mottled drab brown glazed creampan
    1 mottled salmon glazed creampan
    1 mottled grayish brown glazed creampan
    1 mottled brown and green glazed creampan
    1 mottled maroon glazed creampan

1 mottled drab brown glazed creampan
1 unglazed pink vessel
1 maroon-black glazed vessel
—
27

Indian Pottery:

5 orange to black sand-tempered plain flat rim Indian pots
1 red-orange notched rim dish
—
6

Tobacco Pipes:

1 heel fragment marked *TD*
1 "rib" molded bowl
1 brown glazed bit
1 small spur

Wine Bottles (see fig. 46):

2 type 1
1 type 2
6 type 4
4 type 5 and 6
3 type 7 and 15 Necks and Bases
1 type 14
———
5 bases type 1–5 Necks
2 bases type 5 and 6
1 base type 17
—
25

1 case bottle
1 square pale blue-green bottle

Miscellaneous Glassware:

1 teardrop wineglass
1 clear glass tumbler
1 TURLINGTON'S BALSOM OF LIFE medicine bottle
2 cylindrical green pharmaceutical bottles
1 cylindrical clear glass pharmaceutical bottle
1 clear etched drinking glass or rummer

Tools

1 large axe
1 hatchet

    1 spade
    1 broad hoe
    1 narrow hoe
    1 half-round file
    1 triangular file

Stable and Barn Equipment:

    2 saddles (?)
    1 curb bridle bit and harness
    2 bells

House Implements and Hardware:

    2 T-hinges
    1 trunk
    1 door lock
    1 padlock
    1 iron cauldron
    3 pot hooks
    1 adjustable chimney crane
    1 brass candlestick

Appendix E

A LIST OF MARINES UNDER COMMAND
OF CAPTAIN NOBLE JONES
29 SEPTEMBER 1741 *

To Noble Jones 6 mon pay as Commander of the Boat with 10
Marines to Guard the Inland Passages of the Rivers Savannah &
Ogeechee 20/–/–

Wm. Evans " , Serj & Coxswain "		10/10/–
To Midi, Miller, Rich Talley, Alex Ross & John Boyd as Marines		36/–/–
To James Scott 5 & 8		8/–/–
" John Smally 4		6/–/–
" James Anderson 2 & for his Servant Edw. Davison		3/–/–
To Thomas Wilkins 8 & Servant Watkins		8/–/–
To James Burnside 3 Serv. G. Howe		4/2/6
To Rich Wilkins 1 7 marine		1/17/–
To Pat Cardiff 1 7 10		2/–/–
To Jean Stuart (?) 4 18 for like pay of Donald Stuart dec^d to Aug 4' last		6/18/–
To Wm. Eame (?) 1 10		2/6/8

* "The Account of General James Oglethorpe, 1738–1743," Georgia Historical Society, Savannah, Ga.

 *Notes*

I: DOCUMENTARY HISTORY

1. E. Merton Coulter, *Wormsloe*, p. 21.
2. Allen D. Candler, ed., *The Colonial Records of the State of Georgia*, 4:618–19.
3. Coulter, *Wormsloe*, p. 21.
4. George Wymberly Jones DeRenne, "Notes Concerning Noble Jones," University of Georgia Libraries, Athens.
5. Candler, *Colonial Records*, 4:652.
6. Phillips Collection of the Earl of Egmont Papers, typescript, University of Georgia Libraries, vol. 14205–2, no. 206 (343).
7. Edward Kimber, "Itenerant Observations in America," p. 15.
8. The submission of this map is mentioned in Candler, *Colonial Records*, 26:347–48. The map itself is entitled: "A Map of Savannah River beginning at Stone-Bluff . . ."
9. Kimber, "Itenerant Observations," p. 7.
10. Candler, *Colonial Records*, 4:637.
11. "The Account of General James Oglethorpe, 1738–1743," Georgia Historical Society, Savannah.
12. Candler, *Colonial Records*, 4:652.
13. "Account of Oglethorpe," 29 September 1740.
14. Candler, *Colonial Records*, 30:229.
15. Ibid., 4, sup.:14.
16. Ibid., p. 174.
17. Phillips Collection, vol. 14205–2, no. 206 (343).
18. Photograph of Noble Jones's will in Coulter, *Wormsloe*, pp. 104–5.
19. "Noble Jones, Noble Wimberly Jones, George Jones Letter Book," University of Georgia Libraries, Athens.
20. John Bartram, "Diary of a Journey Through the Carolinas, Georgia, and Florida from July 1, 1765 to April 10, 1766," pp. 30, 66.

21. *Georgia Gazette,* 11 July 1765.

22. Bartram, "Diary of a Journey," pp. 30, 66.

23. Coulter, *Wormsloe,* pp. 104–5. Noble Jones's remains were subsequently moved to the Colonial Cemetery in Savannah, then later laid to rest at Bonaventure Cemetery in the same city.

24. Ibid., pp. 106–7.

25. Archibald Campbell, "Sketch of the Northern Frontiers of Georgia, 1780."

26. Noble Wimberly Jones to Jona Homer, 1797, "Jones Letter Book," p. 7.

27. Sarah Jones to George Jones, 18 November 1796, ibid., p. 12.

28. Noble Wimberly Jones to George Jones, 25 August 1804, ibid., p. 14; and Coulter, *Wormsloe,* p. 181.

29. Coulter, *Wormsloe,* p. 207.

30. Contract between George Jones and John Rawls entered 2 January 1810, Chatham County; University of Georgia Libraries, Athens.

31. Lease of George Jones to Ann Reid entered 8 February 1819, Chatham County; University of Georgia Libraries, Athens.

32. John McKinnon, Map of Chatham County, 1816.

33. Coulter, *Wormsloe,* p. 207.

34. Letter of agreement between George Jones and Alexander J. C. Shaw, 25 July 1828, University of Georgia Libraries, Athens. The author is indebted to Craig Barrow, Jr., Eudora Roebling, and John Bonner for locating this document.

II: ARCHAEOLOGY

1. Ivor Noël Hume, *A Guide to the Artifacts of Colonial America,* p. 65.

2. The sherds were without decoration, plain drab white, and no larger than ½″ in size; therefore, they were not illustrated. However, they must have come from a cup similar to that illustrated in Ivor Noël Hume, "Excavations at Rosewell, Gloucester County, Virginia, 1951–1959," p. 208, fig. 27, no. 10.

3. Ivor Noël Hume, *Here Lies Virginia,* pp. 296, 299. Until further archaeological and historical research is conducted into the ceramics of eighteenth-century Georgia, one must assume that

what has been found to be true in Virginia may well have been true for the colonies to the south.

4. The J. C. Harrington and Lewis Binford method of dating tobacco pipe stems by hole diameter is explained in Noël Hume, *Artifacts,* pp. 297–302.

5. Ibid., p. 300. A study made of pipe stem collections from Williamsburg suggests that a thousand samples must be measured to arrive at a consistently accurate date.

6. A similar border motif is illustrated in F. H. Garner, *English Delftware,* plates 80A and 86.

7. See chapter 1, note 33.

III: ARCHITECTURE

1. Fredrick Doveton Nichols, *The Early Architecture of Georgia,* p. 26.

2. Francis Moore, "A Voyage to Georgia Begun in the Year 1735," pp. 44, 114.

3. Albert Manucy, "Specifications for a Scale Model of the Town of Frederica in Georgia about 1742," p. 23.

4. "Extracts from the Journal of the Trustees Palace Court," 19 January 1733–1734. Quoted in Nichols, *Architecture of Georgia,* p. 26.

5. Peter Gordon, "A View of Savannah as it Stood the 29th of March, 1734," University of Georgia Libraries, Athens.

6. Nichols, *Architecture of Georgia,* p. 26.

7. Manucy, "Specifications," pp. 16–17.

8. Peter Gordon, "A View of Savannah."

9. Moore, "A Voyage to Georgia," p. 93.

10. Ibid., p. 94.

11. Ibid., p. 106.

12. Candler, *Colonial Records,* 39:473.

13. Nichols, *Architecture of Georgia,* p. 2.

14. Manucy, "Specifications," p. 17.

15. Moore, "A Voyage to Georgia," p. 94.

16. Manucy, "Specifications," p. 17.

17. Ibid., p. 18.

18. "Journal of the Earl of Egmont," 9 February 1741–1742, in Candler, *Colonial Records,* 5:591.

19. Verner W. Crane, *The Southern Frontier,* p. 189; Marmaduke Floyd, "Certain Tabby Ruins of the Georgia Coast," in Coulter, *Georgia's Disputed Ruins,* p. 63.

20. Albert C. Manucy, "American Notes," p. 32.

21. Albert C. Manucy, *The Houses of St. Augustine,* p. 33.

22. Bartram, "Diary of a Journey," quoted at length in Manucy, *St. Augustine,* pp. 32–33.

23. In the "Account of Oglethorpe" several entries refer to the wages paid to various laborers and carpenters for duties performed during "tappy" (tabby) construction at Fort Frederica, thus providing eighteenth-century terms for various equipment used in the tabby process. For example, an entry for 14 February 1740 states: "To Tho Walker for making Tappy Boxes and Needles for ye Barracks [paid] 9 shillings 9 prnvr" and 20 February 1740: "To Tho Walker for making Needles for the Tappy Boxes, [paid] 6 shillings."

24. It is the contention of Marmaduke Floyd that wide courses were used in eighteenth-century tabby construction while during the revival of tabby work in the early nineteenth century, courses of one foot or less were used. See Floyd, "Certain Tabby Ruins," in Coulter, *Georgia's Disputed Ruins.*

25. Manucy, *St. Augustine,* p. 69.

26. Manucy, "Specifications," p. 25; *St. Augustine,* p. 67.

27. Floyd, "Certain Tabby Ruins," p. 70.

28. Letter from Thomas Spalding of Sapelo Island, Ga. to N. C. Whiting, 29 July 1844, quoted in Floyd, "Certain Tabby Ruins," pp. 74–75.

29. There are at least forty tabby ruins on Ossabaw Island, Ga., alone.

30. Manucy, *St. Augustine,* p. 62.

31. Ibid.

32. Manucy, "Specifications," p. 19. See figs. 10, 12, 31, and 33.

33. Everette J. Fauber, "A Comprehensive Report and a Proposal for the Restoration of Captain Horton's House on Jekyll Island, Georgia, 1967," fig. 6.

34. Manucy, *St. Augustine,* figs. 25, 35.

35. No documents of the Spanish period referring to one-and-a-half-story houses were available. However, an Englishman described the ruined old house he purchased as being 16' high which

is far too high for a one-story house and not high enough for a two-story. Manucy, *St. Augustine,* p. 116.

36. Ibid., p. 67.

37. Manucy, "Specifications," p. 27.

38. Fauber, "Horton House," p. 79. Late nineteenth-century "restoration" of these ruins have made it difficult to measure accurately the original wall height.

39. Manucy, *St. Augustine,* p. 70; "Specifications," p. 27; Fauber, "Horton House," p. 44.

40. Manucy, *St. Augustine,* pp. 118–19, and fig. 73.

41. Manucy, "Specifications," p. 36.

42. Fauber, "Horton House," pp. 45–46.

43. Manucy, *St. Augustine,* p. 81.

44. Manucy, "Specifications," p. 29.

45. Fauber, "Horton House," pp. 65–67.

46. Manucy, *St. Augustine,* pp. 98–99.

47. Manucy, "Specifications," p. 35.

48. Fauber, "Horton House," fig. 6.

49. Manucy, *St. Augustine,* p. 80.

50. Manucy, "Specifications," figs. 10, 12, 15, 31, 33, 34.

51. See note 42 above.

52. Manucy, *St. Augustine,* figs. 25, 35.

53. Ibid., pp. 86–89.

54. Manucy, "Specifications," p. 30, and figs. 10, 12, 15, 31, 32, 34.

55. Manucy, *St. Augustine,* p. 89.

56. Manucy, "Specifications," pp. 31, 59.

57. Manucy, *St. Augustine,* pp. 109–110.

58. Manucy, "Specifications," p. 32.

59. Fauber, "Horton House," p. 25, fig. 3; p. 124, fig. 37.

60. Manucy, *St. Augustine,* pp. 115, 116, and fig. 35.

61. Manucy, "Specifications," passim.

62. Fauber, "Horton House," p. 124, fig. 37.

63. Nichols, *Architecture of Georgia,* p. 2.

64. Kimber, "Itenerant Observations," p. 15.

65. Manucy, *St. Augustine,* p. 57, fig. 25D.

66. Ibid. Manucy recounts the construction of wooden floors for flour barrel storage built in Florida in 1745.

67. Ibid., fig. 57. At least thirteen different moldings were used at St. Augustine alone.

68. Bartram, "Diary of a Journey," pp. 30, 66.

69. In a letter to the Trustees, 29 December 1739, Oglethorpe stated: "I Therefore began to fortify Frederica and inclose the whole town . . . It is half a Hexagon with two bastions and two half Bastions and Towers after Monsieur Vauban's method." In *Collections of the Georgia Historical Society,* 3:100. Jones probably followed the Vauban method at the fort also. See Sebastian Vauban, *A New Treatise of Fortification,* fig. A.

70. For similar square-hipped roof outbuildings, see Nichols, *Architecture of Georgia,* pp. 145, 180, 188. One example made of tabby stands at the eighteenth-century Button Gwinnett House on St. Catherine's Island, Ga. See fig. 33.

71. Letter from Thomas Spalding quoted in Floyd, "Certain Tabby Ruins," pp. 74–75.

72. Jones was commanded by Oglethorpe "to raise ten men for a Guard and Scout Boat" sometime before 8 August 1740. See Candler, *Colonial Records,* 4:637. The pay records indicate that they remained under his command at least until 1744 and probably until 1748 or 1749 when the troops were disbanded.

73. Phillips Collection, vol. 14206, no. 93 (140).

74. Anthony N. B. Garvan, *Architecture and Town Planning in Colonial Connecticut,* p. 127, fig. 57.

IV: THE ARTIFACTS

1. C. Wilson Peck, *English Copper, Tin and Bronze Coins in the British Museum, 1558–1958,* p. 212.

2. E. Merton Coulter, ed., *The Journal of William Stephens,* 2:81.

3. Letter from Professor Adams, 21 September 1970.

4. See appendix A.

V: ARTIFACT ILLUSTRATIONS

1. There is a good possibility that this piece was locally made. A potter with apprentices was working in Savannah as early as 1738. See E. D. Wells, "Duche, the Potter," pp. 383–90.

2. Similar rolled rims illustrated in Ivor Noël Hume, "Excavations at Tutter's Neck in James City County, Virginia, 1960–61," p. 68, fig. 19, nos. 3 and 4; and C. Malcolm Watkins and Ivor

Noël Hume, "The 'Poor Potter' of Yorktown," p. 100, fig. 13, no. 3.

3. Sherds of this ware were found throughout the site, usually in levels associated with the tabby construction. A large unglazed bottle in Williamsburg in an archaeological context of ca. 1765 is illustrated in Noël Hume, "The 'Poor Potter' of Yorktown," p. 106, fig. 18.

4. A similar example from a waster dump of Rudolph Krist, who operated in Bethabara from 1770 to ca. 1800, is illustrated in Stanley South, "Photography in Historical Archaeology," p. 97, fig. 2, right.

5. The fact that this bottle was found in such a late archaeological context and that the mask may be absent suggests the date. Noël Hume, *Artifacts,* p. 57.

6. Outline form and dating information is based on a similar example illustrated and described in Ivor Noël Hume, "Excavations at Rosewell, Gloucester County, Virginia, 1957–59," p. 186, fig. 13, no. 1; and p. 205, fig. 26, no. 7.

7. A similar example, found in a context of the 1740s, is on display at Fort Frederica National Monument Museum, Fort Frederica, St. Simons, Ga.

8. A saucer with same pattern was found in a 1763–1772 context in Virginia. Noël Hume, "Excavations at Rosewell," p. 181, fig. 11, no. 4.

9. A similar piece is illustrated in Noël Hume, "Excavations at Rosewell," p. 181, fig. 11, no. 4.

10. Probably similar to basin illustrated in Noël Hume, "Excavations at Rosewell," p. 205, fig. 26, no. 3.

11. Various similar jar shapes dating from the 1680s through the eighteenth century are illustrated in Geoffrey Eliot Howard, *Early English Drug Jars;* G. Bernard Hughes, *English and Scottish Earthenware, 1660–1860,* p. 22, suggests that delftware with a pinkish cast was made at Lambeth.

12. A similar vessel dated to the period 1680–1780 is illustrated in Noël Hume, *Artifacts,* p. 205, fig. 67, no. 5.

13. The presence of the cherub-decorated sherd which may have come from the same vessel suggests that it may have been a drug jar. However, the footring is shaped more like a cup base. Similar cherub motifs found in archaeological context of ca. 1720 are illustrated in Noël Hume, *Artifacts,* p. 207, fig. 68.

14. Similar example mentioned is illustrated in Charles J. Lomax, *Quaint Old English Pottery*, plate 30.

15. Similar example mentioned is illustrated in John E. Hodgkin, *Examples of Early English Pottery Named, Dated and Inscribed*, p. 37, no. 128. The piece is inscribed: *John Simpson, 1735*.

16. A similarly decorated dish attributed to Staffordshire and dated "early eighteenth century" is illustrated in Reginald G. Haggar, *English Country Pottery*, p. 64, plate 1A.

17. Sherd with similar pattern attributed to 1725–1750 is illustrated in Noël Hume, *Artifacts*, p. 107, fig. 29, upper right.

18. According to G. Bernard Hughes, *English and Scottish Earthenware, 1660–1860*, p. 50, this tea ware was being produced by 1740.

19. This particular floral motif and chevron rouletting on scratch blue ware must have been common. For vessels with this design, see Hodgkin, *Examples of Early English Pottery*, p. 157, no. 577 (dated by inscription 23 July 1761); William Louis Calver and Reginald Pelham Bolton, *History Written with Pick and Shovel*, p. 244, fig. 5; and Noël Hume, *Artifacts*, p. 117, fig. 36 (dated ca. 1760–1775).

20. Identical molded plates are illustrated in Noël Hume, "Excavations at Rosewell," p. 206, fig. 27, no. 14 (dated 1745–1760), and in Edwin Atlee Barber, *Saltglazed Stoneware*, opposite page 18, nos. 27–29 (dated about 1750).

21. Similar larger example without knob but with same beveled edge is illustrated in Noël Hume, "Excavations at Rosewell," p. 206, fig. 27, no. 8.

22. This border pattern illustrated in Noël Hume, *Artifacts*, p. 116, fig. 35, no. 2.

23. Dating information for this type of pottery is available in Audrey Noël Hume, "Some Ceramic Milestones of Use to the Archaeologist," *The Journal of the Society for Post-Medieval Archaeology*, 2:163. The barley pattern is illustrated in Noël Hume, *Artifacts*, p. 116, fig. 35, no. 3.

24. The Royal pattern is illustrated and the dating of creamware is discussed in Noël Hume, *Artifacts*, p. 116.

25. A similar fluted vase lid without the green edge is illustrated in Geoffrey Wills, *English Pottery and Porcelain*, p. 126, fig. 119, center (dated 1765).

26. Noël Hume, *Artifacts,* p. 126.

27. Donald C. Towner, *English Cream-Coloured Earthenware,* fig. 34B, illustrates a teapot featuring an identical hand-painted design in the same colors with "pearl" beaded rims attributed to Leeds, 1775. This particular type of handle and terminal was made only at Leeds and possibly Swinton in the period ca. 1775–1815. See Towner, p. 69, fig. 4, no. 8.

28. A creamware mug with a similar scene and verse is presently on display in the Victoria and Albert Museum, cat. no. 1265–1919, dated to the early nineteenth century. Letter from Ivor Noël Hume, Director, Department of Archaeology, Colonial Williamsburg, Inc., 7 May 1970.

29. Vessels with similar rolled rims illustrated in Hughes, *English and Scottish Earthenware,* plates 7 and 8.

30. Similar marbled decoration illustrated in Susan Van Rensselaer, "Banded Creamware," *Antiques Magazine* 90 (September 1966) :340, top; and Robert J. Sim, "Banded Creamware," *Antiques Magazine* 85 (August 1945) :fig. 5. For dating information see Noël Hume, *Artifacts,* p. 131.

31. Exactly when the transfer-printed willow pattern was first used on pearlware is not known. Griselda Lewis in *A Picture History of English Pottery* illustrates a willow pattern service attributed to 1790–1793. According to Noël Hume, *Artifacts,* p. 130, the only known dated piece is marked: *Thomasine Willey, 1818.*

32. An identical marked base is illustrated in Noël Hume, *Artifacts,* p. 263, fig. 85. Buddhist symbols on Chinese porcelain are illustrated in George Savage, *Porcelain Through the Ages,* p. 96.

33. For a discussion of dry body redware, see Noël Hume, *Artifacts,* pp. 120–21.

34. A mug with a similar rim design attributed to Liverpool about 1750 is illustrated in Garner, *English Delftware,* plate 75A.

35. See Noël Hume, *Artifacts,* pp. 109–111.

36. This shape is a transitional form between the squat early bottles of the late seventeenth century and early eighteenth century and the cylindrical bottles of the later eighteenth century. Similar bottles dated 1731 and 1735 are illustrated in Noël Hume, *Artifacts,* pp. 64–65. Two bottles of similar shape were also found in an archaeological context of 1763–1772 in Virginia. Noël Hume, "Excavations at Rosewell," p. 213, fig. 30, nos. 5 and 7.

37. All bottle manufacturing dates hereafter are based on bottles illustrated in Ivor Noël Hume, "The Glass Wine Bottle in Colonial Virginia," *Journal of Glass Studies* 3 (1961): pp. 99–101, and *Artifacts*, pp. 63–68, figs. 8–13.

38. Dating based on string rim only. The author has never seen an example of a round shouldered bottle with such a rim; therefore the dating is conjectural.

39. Reconstruction based on restored vessel illustrated in Noël Hume, "The Glass Wine Bottle," p. 106, fig. 6, left.

40. Ibid.

41. Dating is based on type illustrated in Noël Hume, *Artifacts*, p. 191, fig. 64, no. 17. A similar stem found in a 1763–1772 archaeological context is illustrated in Noël Hume, "Excavations at Rosewell," p. 217, fig. 32, nos. 6 and 7.

42. Ibid.

43. A similar piece is illustrated in Noël Hume, *Artifacts*, p. 191, fig. 64, no. 18; and "A Collection of Glass from Port Royal, Jamaica," p. 28, fig. 12, no. 43; and p. 30, fig. 13, nos. 47 and 48.

44. According to G. Bernard Hughes, *English, Scottish and Irish Table Glass*, pp. 142–43, these simple patterns were initially engraved in factories after 1760. Hughes also illustrates several bucket bowl engraved drinking glasses, goblets, and rummers dating in the period 1760–1820 (pp. 189–196, figs. 131–151).

45. Hughes attributes tumblers with sloping sides, round faceted bodies, and cut bottoms to that period (after ca. 1740). Ibid., pp. 334–35.

46. Ibid.

47. Hughes illustrates wineglasses which may have been the type to which this example belongs (p. 101, fig. 55, fig. 62) although the small beaded teardrops are often found on decanter stoppers of the early eighteenth century (p. 278, fig. 210). See Noël Hume, "Glass from Port Royal," p. 30, fig. 13, no. 49; and *Artifacts*, p. 197, fig. 65, no. 7.

48. Conjectural shape is based on intact example illustrated in W. B. Honey, *Glass*, plate 50A. This bottle was found at Golden Savane, London, and is attributed to the seventeenth century. See also Noël Hume, "Excavations at Rosewell," fig. 33, no. 1.

49. The actual inscription was so corroded and poorly molded that it was largely unreadable; the conjectural shape, inscription,

and dating are based on Noël Hume, *Here Lies Virginia,* p. 273, fig. 110, and "Glass in Colonial Williamsburg's Archaeological Collections," pp. 43–44.

50. See Noël Hume, *Artifacts,* p. 73, fig. 17, nos. 11 and 13.

51. A similar buckle is illustrated in John L. Cotter, *Archaeological Excavations at Jamestown, Virginia,* p. 190, plate 88.

52. See Noël Hume, *Artifacts,* p. 85, plate 20, no. 12.

53. A similar buckle is illustrated in Noël Hume, "Excavations at Rosewell," p. 228, fig. 38, no. 9.

54. Similar examples are illustrated in J. Seymour Lindsay, *Iron and Brass Implements of the English and American House,* figs. 266, 268, 270.

55. For dating characteristics of knives, see Noël Hume, *Artifacts,* p. 182, fig. 63.

56. Ibid.

57. Similar knives with bone handles are illustrated in Eugene T. Peterson, *Gentlemen on the Frontier,* p. 30, lower right, and p. 58, fourth column, top.

58. Ibid.

59. Noël Hume, "Excavations at Rosewell," p. 197, fig. 21, no. 5.

60. A similar bowl is illustrated in Noël Hume, "Excavations at Tutter's Neck," p. 38, fig. 15, no. 11.

61. For a discussion of the datable characteristics of latten spoons, see Noël Hume, *Artifacts,* p. 183.

62. Ibid., p. 180.

63. Ibid., p. 303, fig. 97, no. 18.

64. This was found with a notched rim slipware dish (fig. 48, no. 17). It was probably made by either the Indians or the colonists in an attempt to copy the Staffordshire types in native clay.

65. It is possible that this vessel was made during the last period of occupation of the protohistoric Indian occupation of the Savannah area. See Joseph Caldwell and Catherine McCann, *Irene Mound Site, Chatham County, Georgia.*

66. Various types of English and French gunflints are discussed and illustrated in Noël Hume, *Artifacts,* pp. 220–21; and Harold L. Peterson, *Arms and Armor in Colonial America, 1526–1783,* pp. 228–29, plate 216.

67. But according to Peterson, p. 229, "No flints were produced in America." Peterson probably meant commercially. If not, the Wormslow flints must be unique.

68. The dragonesque decorative sideplate was commonly used on firearms from the late seventeenth to the mid-nineteenth century, the earlier examples engraved. Muskets with this symbol were given or traded to the Indians and thus are usually referred to as "Indian trade guns." See Noël Hume, *Artifacts*, pp. 217–18. A "Whateley" gun of early nineteenth century date and a series of drawings illustrating dragonesque plates appear in Carl P. Russel, *Guns on the Early Frontiers*, p. 119, fig. 25, e and f; and fig. 27. John Whatley is listed as a gunsmith in London in Ian Glen-Denning, *British Pistols and Guns, 1640–1840*, appendix.

69. The dating of this and the buttons which follow is based on similar examples found at Brunswicktown, N.C., either in a context of 1726–1776 or in a context of 1800–1830, illustrated in Noël Hume, *Artifacts*, p. 91, fig. 23.

70. Ibid. See also Calver and Bolton, *History Written with Pick and Shovel*, p. 103, plate 8.

71. Similar designs on buttons are illustrated in Petersen, *Gentlemen on the Frontier*, p. 59.

72. A similar boss ⅛" larger is illustrated in Noël Hume, "Excavations at Rosewell," p. 195, no. 6.

73. Several of these bale seals usually attached to shipments of cloth and in a revolutionary war context are discussed and illustrated in Calver and Bolton, *History Written with Pick and Shovel*, pp. 264–75.

74. Similar iron hoes found in Virginia in an archaeological context of 1763–1772. Noël Hume, "Excavations at Rosewell," p. 227, fig. 37, no. 3.

75. A felling axe with similar characteristics but with square eye and square bit, dated after 1725, is illustrated in Ralph Hodgkinson, *Tools of the Woodworker*, p. 12, fig. 8.

76. One of three flatirons recovered at the site. (13A) Pit C. (30M)

77. See Thomas K. Bullock, *The Wigmaker in Eighteenth Century Williamsburg*, p. 12, fig. 22.

78. An identical implement labeled "nippers" is on display at the Barracks, Frederica National Monument, St. Simon's, Ga.

Possibly used in shoemaking. See Harold B. Gill, *The Leather-worker in Eighteenth-Century Williamsburg*, p. 25, fig. 2.

79. Similar dividers are illustrated in Noël Hume, "Excavations at Tutter's Neck," p. 58, fig. 15, no. 18; and Cotter, *Excavations at Jamestown*, p. 174, plate 72.

80. Similar objects are illustrated in Noël Hume, "Excavations at Clay Bank in Gloucester County, Virginia, 1962–1963," p. 20, fig. 13, nos. 1 and 2; "Excavations at Tutter's Neck," p. 61, fig. 16, no. 12; and "Excavations at Rosewell," p. 224, fig. 36, no. 8.

81. Similar bolts are shown in Noël Hume, *Artifacts*, p. 248, fig. 77B, nos. 1 and 2.

82. Padlock. A similar lock is illustrated in Noël Hume, *Artifacts*, p. 251, fig. 80, left.

83. Plate stock locks illustrated in Noël Hume, *Artifacts*, p. 248, fig. 77B, nos. 1 and 2.

84. A similar back plate found in an eighteenth-century context in Virginia is illustrated in C. Malcolm Watkins, *The Cultural History of Marlborough, Virginia*, p. 169, fig. 91D. The placement of this piece and no. 2 and no. 3 below is strictly conjectural and probably oversimplified.

85. Horn saddle pommels are generally thought to be contemporary with the cattle boom in the American West of the last three-quarters of the nineteenth century. All of the saddle parts were found in the well trash (pit C), but since the pommel and the front plates were found apart, they were probably not both on the same saddle. They are drawn together only to illustrate their position.

86. Front plates are commonly found on colonial sites. One example (somewhat larger) found by the author in Virginia in an archaeological context of 1690–1710 is illustrated in William M. Kelso, "More Excavations at Lightfoot," p. 67, fig. 12, no. 2.

87. The author has found similar cheekpieces with shorter arms in a late seventeenth-century context; see William M. Kelso, "Excavations of a Late Seventeenth Century Domestic Refuse Pit Near Lightfoot in James City County, Virginia, 1964–65," p. 109, fig. e, nos. 1 and 2. An identical curb bit is illustrated in Noël Hume, *Artifacts*, p. 241, fig. 75, no. 5.

88. Bells of this type are probably undatable in that they have been made from the seventh century to the twentieth century. See

Satis N. Coleman, *The Book of Bells,* p. 23; and American Bell Association, *Bells of the World,* pp. 112, 120. A cowbell of similar shape was sold by Sears, Roebuck Company in 1902; the price ranged from ten cents to twenty-eight cents apiece. *Sears, Roebuck Catalogue: 1902 Edition,* p. 566.

89. The unusual shape may suggest that this bell was made in France; the author has seen one of similar shape of French manufacture dating from the late nineteenth century in the possession of Mrs. Elfrida DeRenne Barrow, Savannah, Georgia.

90. Perhaps this piece was made by the blacksmith who used a similar heart-shaped mark on the axehead; see fig. 51, no. 6 above.

91. The object's archaeological context suggests that this chain and hook may have been used to suspend the 50 lb. lead weight shown in fig. 40 above.

92. A similar bolt with a rectangular shaft is illustrated in Noël Hume, "Excavations at Rosewell," p. 223, fig. 36, no. 10.

93. Similar plates are shown in Noël Hume, "Excavations at Rosewell," p. 223, fig. 36, nos. 12 and 13.

94. A similar iron hook with wire still in situ, apparently a bell wire support, is illustrated in Helen Sutermeister, "An Eighteenth-Century Urban Estate in New France," p. 114, fig. 45, no. 12.

95. A similar spike is illustrated in Sutermeister, no. 10.

96. A chimney crane arm (for hanging pots at different levels) with notched adjustments and a scrolled terminal is illustrated in J. Seymour Lindsay, *Iron and Brass Implements,* fig. 30. It is also possible that this piece is the sideplate from a grating.

97. Such vessels usually had short triangular tripod legs. Several of these legs were found in pit C (30D, 30E, 30M) varying in size from 2″ to $2\frac{11}{24}$″ in length. Cauldrons are illustrated in Lindsey, figs. 111–24.

 *Bibliography*

PUBLISHED SOURCES

American Bell Association. *Bells of the World*. Marietta, Ga.: Darby and Maddox, 1963.

Barber, William Atlee. *Saltglazed Stoneware*. New York: Doubleday, Page, and Co., 1907.

Bartram, John. "Diary of a Journey through the Carolinas, Georgia, and Florida from July 1, 1765 to April 10, 1766." Edited by Francis Harper. In *Transactions of the American Philosophical Society* (Philadelphia, 1942), new series, vol. 33, pt. 1, pp. 30–66.

Bullock, Thomas K., and Tonkin, Maurice B., Jr. *The Wigmaker in Eighteenth-Century Williamsburg*. Williamsburg Craft Series. Williamsburg, Va.: Colonial Williamsburg, 1967.

Caldwell, Joseph, and McCann, Catherine. *Irene Mound Site, Chatham County, Georgia*. Savannah, Ga.: Works Project Administration, 1941.

Calver, William Louis, and Bolton, Reginald Pelham. *History Written with Pick and Shovel*. New York: New York Historical Society, 1950.

Candler, Allen D., ed. *The Colonial Records of the State of Georgia*. 26 vols. Atlanta, 1904–1916.

Candler, Allen D., ed. *The Colonial Records of the State of Georgia*. WPA Project No. 3750, 1937–1941.

Coleman, Satis N. *The Book of Bells*. New York: John Day Co., 1938.

Cotter, John L. *Archaeological Excavations at Jamestown, Virginia*. Washington, D.C.: National Park Service, 1958.

Coulter, E. Merton. *Georgia's Disputed Ruins*. Chapel Hill: University of North Carolina Press, 1937.

———. *The Journal of William Stephens*. 3 vols. Athens: University of Georgia Press, 1958.

Coulter, E. Merton. *Wormsloe: Two Centuries of a Georgia Family.* Athens: University of Georgia Press, 1955.

Crane, Verner W. *The Southern Frontier.* Durham, N.C.: Duke University Press, 1928.

Forman, Henry Chandlee. *The Architecture of the Old South: The Medieval Style, 1585–1850.* Cambridge, Mass.: Harvard University Press, 1948.

Garner, F. H. *English Delftware.* New York: Van Nostrand Co., 1948.

Garvan, Anthony N. B. *Architecture and Town Planning in Colonial Connecticut.* New Haven: Yale University Press, 1951.

Gill, Harold B., and Townsend, Raymond R. *The Leatherworker in Eighteenth-Century Williamsburg.* Williamsburg Craft Series. Williamsburg, Va.: Colonial Williamsburg, 1967.

Glen-Denning, Ian. *British Pistols and Guns, 1640–1840.* New York: Arco Publishing Co., 1951.

Haggar, Reginald G. *English Country Pottery.* London: Phoenix House, 1950.

Hodgkin, John Eliot, and Hodgkin, Edith. *Examples of Early English Pottery Named, Dated and Inscribed.* London: Cassell and Co., 1941.

Hodgkinson, Ralph. *Tools of the Woodworker.* Technical Leaflet 28. Nashville: American Association for State and Local History, n.d.

Honey, W. B. *English Pottery and Porcelain.* London: A. & C. Black, 1952.

————. *Glass: A Handbook for the Study of Glass Vessels of All Periods and Countries.* London: Victoria and Albert Museum, 1946.

Howard, Geoffrey Eliot. *Early English Drug Jars.* London: The Medici Society, 1931.

Hughes, G. Bernard. *English and Scottish Earthenware, 1660–1860.* London: Abbey Fine Arts, n.d.

————. *English, Scottish, and Irish Table Glass.* New York: Bramhall House, 1956.

"James Oglethorpe to the Trustees, December 29, 1739." In *Collections of the Georgia Historical Society,* vol. 3, p. 100.

Kelso, William M. "Excavation of a Late Seventeenth Century Domestic Refuse Pit in James City County, Virginia, 1964–

1965." *Quarterly Bulletin, Archaeological Society of Virginia* 20 (June 1966) :109.

————. "More Excavations at Lightfoot: Another Late Seventeenth Century Domestic Refuse Pit in James City County, Virginia." *Quarterly Bulletin, Archaeological Society of Virginia* 22 (December 1967) :67.

Kimber, Edward. "Itenerant Observations in America," reprinted from *London Magazine, 1745–46.* In *Collections of the Georgia Historical Society,* vol. 4 (1878), appendix 1–64.

Lewis, Griselda. *A Picture History of English Pottery.* New York: Macmillan, 1956.

Lindsay, J. Seymour. *Iron and Brass Implements of the English and American House.* London: Portland Press, 1927.

Lomax, Charles J. *Quaint Old English Pottery.* London: Sheratt and Hughes, 1909.

Manucy, Albert C. "American Notes." *Society of Architectural Historians Journal* 2 (December 1952) :30–32.

————. *The Fort at Frederica.* Tallahassee: Florida State University, 1962.

————. *The Houses of St. Augustine.* Jacksonville: Convention Press, 1962.

Moore, Francis. "A Voyage to Georgia Begun in the Year 1735." In *Collections of the Georgia Historical Society,* vol. 1 (1840).

Nichols, Frederick Dourton. *The Early Architecture of Georgia.* Chapel Hill: University of North Carolina Press, 1951.

Noël Hume, Audrey. "Some Ceramic Milestones of Use to the Archaeologist." *Post Medieval Archaeology* 2 (1969) :163.

Noël Hume, Ivor. "A Collection of Glass from Port Royal, Jamaica." *Historical Archaeology,* vol. 2. Mason, Mich.: Society for Historical Archaeology, 1968.

————. "Excavations at Clay Bank in Gloucester County, Virginia, 1962–1963," *Contributions from the Museum of History and Technology,* paper 52. Washington, D.C.: Smithsonian Institution, 1966.

————. "Excavations at Rosewell, Gloucester County, Virginia, 1957–59," *United States National Museum Bulletin 225.* Washington, D.C.: Smithsonian Institution, 1962.

————. "Excavations at Tutter's Neck in James City County, Virginia, 1960–61," *Contributions from the Museum of History and Technology*. Washington, D.C.: Smithsonian Institution, 1966.

———. *Glass in Colonial Williamsburg's Archaeological Collection*. Colonial Williamsburg's Archaeological Series, no. 1. Williamsburg, Va.: Colonial Williamsburg, 1967.

———. "The Glass Wine Bottle in Colonial Virginia." *Journal of Glass Studies,* vol. 3. Corning, N.Y.: Corning Museum of Glass, 1961.

———. *A Guide to the Artifacts of Colonial America*. New York: Knopf, 1970.

———. *Here Lies Virginia*. New York: Knopf, 1963.

Peck, C. Wilson. *English Copper, Tin and Bronze Coins in the British Museum, 1558–1958*. London: Trustees of the British Museum, 1970.

Petersen, Eugene T. *Gentlemen on the Frontier*. Mackinac Island: Michigan State Park Commission, 1954.

Peterson, Harold L. *Arms and Armor in Colonial America, 1526–1783*. New York: Bramhall House, 1956.

Russel, Carl P. *Guns on the Early Frontiers*. New York: Bonanza Books, 1957.

Savage, George. *Porcelain Through the Ages*. London, 1954.

Sears, Roebuck Catalogue: 1902 Edition. New York: Crown Publishers, 1969.

Sim, Robert J. "Banded Creamware." *Antiques Magazine,* August 1945, pp. 82–83.

South, Stanley A. "Photography in Historical Archaeology." *Historical Archaeology,* vol. 2. Mason, Mich.: Society for Historical Archaeology, 1968.

Sutermeister, Helen. "An Eighteenth-Century Urban Estate in New France." *Post Medieval Archaeology* 2 (1969) :83–118.

Towner, Donald C. *English Cream-Coloured Earthenware*. London: Faber and Faber, n.d.

Van Rensselaer, Susan. "Banded Creamware." *Antiques Magazine,* September 1966, pp. 337–41.

Vauban, Sebastian de. *A New Treatise of Fortification as Practiced by Sebastian de Vauban, Engineer General of France with an Explication of All Terms Appertaining to that Art*. London: Abell Swall, 1693.

Watkins, C. Malcolm. *The Cultural History of Marlborough,*

Virginia. Washington, D.C.: Smithsonian Institution Press, 1968.

————, and Noël Hume, Ivor. "The 'Poor Potter' of Yorktown." *United States National Museum Bulletin 249* (Washington, D.C.: Smithsonian Institution, 1967) .

Wells, E. D. "Duche, The Potter." *Georgia Historical Quarterly* 41 (1957) :383–90.

Wills, Geoffrey. *English Pottery and Porcelain.* London: Guinness Superlatives, 1968.

MANUSCRIPTS

ATHENS, GEORGIA
University of Georgia Libraries, Special Collections

Contract between George Jones and John Rawls, entered 2 January 1810, Chatham County.

DeRenne, George Wymberly Jones. "Notes Concerning Noble Jones."

Lease of George Jones to Ann Reid, entered 8 February 1819, Chatham County.

Letter of Agreement between George Jones and A. S. C. Shaw, 28 July 1826.

"Noble Jones, Noble Wimberly Jones, George Jones Letter Book."

Phillips Collection of the Earl of Egmont Papers. Vol. 14205–2. Typescript.

GAINESVILLE, FLORIDA
University of Florida, Department of Anthropology

Fauber, J. Everette, A.I.A., "A Comprehensive Report and a Proposal for the Restoration of Captain Horton's House on Jekyll Island, Georgia, 1967."

SAVANNAH, GEORGIA
Chatham County Archives

Inventory of Noble Wimberly Jones. File box J, folio 27 (1807) in Ordinary's Office.

Georgia Historical Association

"The Account of General James Oglethorpe, 1738–1743." Microfilm copy. Original manuscript, British Public Record Office, no. 487 AO 3, 119.

ST. SIMON'S ISLAND, GEORGIA
Fort Frederica National Monument

Manucy, Albert. "Specifications for a Scale Model of the Town of Fredrica in Georgia about 1742" (Richmond, Va.: National Park Service, Region One, 1960).

MAPS

Campbell, Archibald. "Sketch of the Northern Frontiers of Georgia." Copy on file in the Georgia Surveyor General Dept., Office of Secretary of State, Atlanta, Ga.

DeBrahm, William Gerard. "A Map of Savannah River beginning at Stone-Bluff . . . Surveyor William Noble of Brahm late Captain Ingenier under his Imperial Majesty Charles II." Faden Collection. No. 45, 1752. Library of Congress, Washington, D.C.

———. "A Map of South Carolina and a Part of Georgia" (London: T. Jeffreys, 1757). Copy on file Georgia Surveyor General Dept., Office of Secretary of State, Atlanta, Ga.

Gordon, Peter. "A View of Savannah as It Stood the 29th of March, 1734." DeRenne Collection. University of Georgia Libraries, Athens, Ga.

Mace, Sanford. "Plan and Elevation of Fort St. Francisco de Pupo." M. Davis Cate Memorial Library, M-18, D-6. Fort Frederica National Monument, St. Simon's Island, Ga.

McKinnon, John. "Map of Chatham County, 1816." Private Collection. Hon. Shelby Myrick, Wild Heron Plantation, Savannah, Ga. Copy on file Chatham County Court House, Savannah, Georgia.

NEWSPAPER

Georgia Gazette (Savannah, 1763–1778). Microfilm copy. Georgia Historical Society, Savannah, Ga.

Index